MAPPING
OUT THE
MILLIONAIRE
MYSTERY

MAPPING
OUT THE
MILLIONAIRE
MYSTERY

Step Into the Secrets of the Wealthy

"THE MONEY COACH"
BRENT KESLER
AND AMERICA'S #1 MONEY MENTOR
CHRIS NAUGLE

Redwood Publishing, LLC

Printed in the United States of America

First Printing, 2020.

Published by:
Redwood Publishing, LLC
Ladera Ranch, CA
www.redwooddigitalpublishing.com

Book Design:
  – Interior Designer: Ghislain Viau
       Charts Designed by it_solution_hub
  – Cover Designer: Michelle Manley

ISBN: 978-1-7344254-0-6 (paperback)
ISBN: 978-1-7344254-1-3 (ebook)

Library of Congress Cataloguing Number: 2020900089

10 9 8 7 6 5 4 3 2 1

Disclaimer

This book has been written solely for informational and educational purposes. No content constitutes professional or individual-specific financial advice. While best efforts were employed when writing this book to include accurate, verifiable content, the author or anyone else who may have been involved in any way in the preparation of this book makes no representations or warranties of any kind and assumes no liabilities as related to the accuracy or completeness of the information presented.

The author and all parties involved in the preparation of this book shall not be held liable for any loss or damages caused, or alleged to have been caused, directly or indirectly, by the information presented herein.

Every individual's financial situation is unique, and the information and strategies in this book speak to the book's audience in general and may not apply to your specific situation. You should always seek the services of a certified financial professional before attempting or implementing any of the strategies detailed in this book.

Register today for your **FREE 10-Part Training**
in

THE
MONEY
MULTIPLIER
METHOD

themoneymultiplier.com/bonus

START HERE

https://themoneymultiplier.com/member-area/

Mapping Out the Millionaire Mystery is a modern,
expanded look at the Infinite Banking Concept™
originally founded by R. Nelson Nash in the early 1980s
as a result of his personal and business journey through
real estate, debt, and work within insurance companies.

Nash has inspired much of the work in this book,
and we have endeavored to take it to the next level
to help you to reclaim control of your money and
find financial freedom in this 21st century.

Read on to discover the impact that
The Money Multiplier Method can have on your life
as you map out the millionaire mystery
and step into the secrets of the wealthy.

Table of Contents

Two Tales of Realization

IT CAN TAKE GREAT FINANCIAL hardship and treading through the muck of a great personal crisis to seek out the financial knowledge that awaits us—the kind that can help us truly step into the secrets of the wealthy.

To help you understand that we are very much on this journey of financial education and the road to financial freedom with you, we'd like to take you back to where we have been—to how we learned what it takes to reclaim control of our finances.

These are our stories of personal realization—ones in which we've worked tirelessly to fund our dreams and fought in the trenches with our debt. Emerging from the tough times of economic downturns and depressions, we have come to build and teach the systems that allow us all to find and reclaim control of the money we need to thrive financially and build long-term wealth.

Brent's Story

For fourteen years, I was a chiropractor and chiropractic coach with several clinics across the Kansas City area. Through those years of working as a chiropractor and opening clinics, I also managed to rack up nearly $1 million in third-party debt.

My love of debt was something that was most definitely not taught to me by my parents. I grew up in Florida in a very close-knit family. My parents had a lot of love, but they weren't the smartest people with money. Dad was a traveling salesman and didn't really do much with checks and credit cards; he was a cash-on-the-fly type of guy. When he'd buy a boat or a car, he'd most often buy them high and sell them low. If he came into a windfall of money, or even a few dollars, he would spend it all. His typical cycle was to spend and then go out and make more money. There were times when we had to sell stuff to get by because the sales weren't coming in, and we had to find a way to pay the rent or the electric bill.

For a period of time, we lived on a trimaran—a three-hulled sailboat. It wasn't a very big space in which to live, but it was home. I clearly remember one occasion when we took the boat from its typical port at the dock and sailed to a local island. On the back of this sailboat was a Zodiac—a rubber raft with a small motor. Since we weren't permitted to bring the boat all the way up to the beach on that island, we put out the anchor, and my mom, my dad, and I got in the little Zodiac and headed off to the island.

As we reached the shore, we walked to the beach on the other side of the island and went for a family swim. All of a sudden, we looked up and saw black smoke rising in the sky. We walked back around to the other side of the island, only to realize that it was *our* boat that was on fire. Before we'd left the boat, Mom had been cooking potatoes. There was grease in the pan and the burner had been left on.

My parents had kept everything they owned on that boat. All Dad's cash (an amount I will never want to know) burned into the ocean. The impact of that day stuck with me for a very long time.

Fast-forward to my life as an adult. After years spent working in sales, I went back to school to become a chiropractor, acquiring my first chiropractic office in 2004. I quickly bought a second office, and eventually a third, fourth, and fifth. I was the owner of five clinics in the Kansas City area, had associate doctors in every clinic, and had racked up far more debt than I was aware of. My kids were thirteen, seven, and five at the time, and I had never taken the time to calculate how much debt I had gotten our family into.

About the same time, a chiropractic mentor of mine named Dr. Enrich told me that I had "to get with his guy" to get my money and finances under control. I sheepishly went to a seminar that "his guy" was putting on, and I paid attention to what he was teaching. It looked and sounded really good, but it also looked too good to be true. I went home, did absolutely nothing, and went back to my daily life: paying bills, racking up debt, and not giving money much thought at all.

Two years later, I returned to a similar financial-education seminar. Ten or twelve of my colleagues who had attended the previous event were there with me once again. They came up to me, ranting and raving about this "banking concept" we had heard about at the seminar two years prior, and how they were using it to build their wealth, maintain control of their finances, and keep their money in their family.

I thought to myself, *there has to be something to this*. There was no way that nearly a dozen of my colleagues were lying to me. Maybe a couple of them, but not *all* of them. In that room in 2008, there was only one difference between them and me: they had implemented the Infinite Banking Concept™ two years prior and I hadn't.

I went home and told my wife, "We've got to start doing this in our life." I then added up all of our debts. $984,711. Almost a million dollars. That's what we owed to third-party creditors for chiropractic offices, student loans, our primary house, a boat, a WaveRunner, and an airplane. In Kansas in 2008, a million in debt was *a lot* of money.

I told my wife we absolutely had to implement this banking concept.

Now, my wife and I are opposites; I am comfortable with acting fast, and she likes to think things through. She has a master's degree in nuclear engineering, so when I came home and said, "We've got to start doing this, and I want to start putting $2,000 a month into our whole life policy," she said, "That's crazy ridiculous!"

We eventually found common ground, started the policy, and then the magic happened. Upon implementing what I now term The Money Multiplier (TMM) Method—our elaboration on R. Nelson Nash's Infinite Banking Concept™—I paid off every penny of the $984,711 in debt in just thirty-nine months. Three years and three months!

What amazed me is that I was able to do it without working any harder, changing my cash flow, or taking any additional risk with our money. All I did was change one step in the process of what I was doing with that money: I became my own banker.

About the same time that I started my banking system, I finally got the audio for R. Nelson Nash's *Becoming Your Own Banker*, and listening to that book changed my life forever. Everything he wrote made so much sense; it fascinated me. Nash and I were both pilots. When he spoke about Infinite Banking, he related it to flying, and I related to him:

I have been flying, as a pilot, for over 53 years, and I learned early on that you could not fly an airplane through a vacuum. It must go through an environment! We have all seen the weather maps with the "HIGHs" and the "LOWs." In the Northern Hemisphere, the HIGHs turn clockwise. A large one can cover 75 percent or more of the U.S.

So picture this situation: You are in Birmingham, AL, with an airplane that can fly 100 miles per hour and your destination is Chicago. The only problem is that you have a headwind of 345 miles per hour! Regardless of what your airspeed indicator says, your airplane is moving toward Miami at 245 miles per hour! If you want to go to Chicago, that's a very good time to get your airplane on the ground—quickly!

Have some patience, and the air mass will move on— they always do. When the HIGH gets directly over the top of you, there is no headwind. You are now covering the ground at 100 mph. And now, the "arrival syndrome" comes into play. You conclude that "you just can't do any better than this. This is the ultimate solution." Nonsense! Have more patience, and the air mass will continue to move on. Now you have a tailwind of 345 M.P.H.! Plus your airplane is moving at a speed of 100 mph. Your ground speed is 445 M.P.H.! That is impressive, isn't it? But, you see, it is much more impressive than most people think. Everything you do in the financial world is compared with what everyone else is doing! Ninety-five percent of the American public is doing the equivalent of flying with a 345 miles per hour headwind. If you have a 345 M.P.H. tailwind, the difference between you and them is twice the wind! That is a difference of 690 M.P.H.!

Most people in this situation concentrate all their attention to trying to make the airplane go 105 M.P.H.! They would do well to spend their energy instead of controlling the environment in which they fly. You can't do that in the airplane world—but you can in the financial world. You can do it by controlling the "banking equation" as it relates to you.

Nash taught that creating our own banking system was like creating a "perpetual tailwind." He stated that while there were (and are) many "financial gurus" out there who speak to our getting out of debt, they do not address the tailwind factor—controlling the financial environment. Nash stated that choosing to control the environment is "the most profitable thing you can do over a lifetime."

Within me was an undeniable passion to share The Money Multiplier Method with others. I became a licensed producer in another office, and five years later, I founded The Money Multiplier, LLC. I'm always looking for the next gig, the next event, because I want to be the guy who is there for that person who is just the same as I was in 2006—hesitant about doing something so new, so outside of the box, that it sounds way too good to be true.

Chris' Story

Over the course of twenty years, I've built and navigated sixteen businesses. Everything that I've been able to create today has come, in large part, to what I've learned first-hand from the financial struggles I faced growing up, and what I endured through the 2000 and 2008 recessions.

I have learned what it takes to build something from next-to-nothing, and I've had to do it several times over in my adult life. In the early 2000s, all of my money was in the stock market, and it vanished when the tech bubble burst. Every penny I made was going back into my skateboard and snowboard business, as I had recently expanded. The banks' lines of credit were my main source of money. When the planes hit the towers in September 2001, so many things went wrong. I had to step back from my business and go get a job as a financial advisor.

I had always been fascinated with making money and with how money works. When I saw the movie *Wall Street*, I was fixated. Working as an advisor was a blessing amid a truly hard time of abandoning my love for my skateboard and snowboard stores. It was when I truly started learning about what life insurance and investments were. My first year in business, at twenty-five years of age, I made $74,000. I started really saving and putting money into life insurance plans long before I knew what Infinite Banking was.

When the market crash hit in 2008, I was a real estate investor, deep into a strip mall development. I had borrowed money from all the wrong people and I was literally one payment away from being bankrupt. My life insurance policies were all loaned out, my 401(k) loans were exhausted, and I had maxed out all of my credit cards.

By the skin of my teeth, I made it through 2008 and started buying real estate again. The only problem was that I was doing it the old-fashioned way. I had no idea how private money worked. I had never really understood that I could just go to other people and borrow money. So I just kept building all these rental properties, and I was working my tail off doing it.

Then, in 2014, I reached thirty-six rental units and went to buy another one, when the bank notified me that I had hit my debt-to-income limit. They froze my lines of credit because they didn't want to loan me any more money. I had made all of my payments on time, and my credit scores were good. I was the proverbial good steward of the banks, but I didn't understand how money really worked. When the bank locked everything up, I couldn't finish renovating the properties I held, and I couldn't make ends meet.

After not being able to buy that next property, things took a turn for the worse. I had to sell *every* property I owned, including the dream house that my wife Lorissa and I had bought and renovated. I couldn't keep the machine going. I knew how to work hard, but I didn't yet know how to work smart and actually build and keep wealth.

The truth is, I have always been great at working hard to make money. Growing up in a lower-middle-class family, I couldn't just ask for something I wanted and get it. Asking my mom, "Hey, can I have twenty bucks?" wasn't an option.

When I was young, my mom would pay me a dollar to do a chore. As a teenager, I was big into BMX, skateboarding, snowboarding, and dirt bikes—activities that all required money. When I wanted skateboard sneakers, a new board, fuel for my dirt bike, or a four-wheeler, I had to go out and mow lawns or clean the neighbor's horse stalls to earn the money to buy them. Making money to get the things I wanted was something that I came to enjoy. I also thought it was what I had to do.

One summer, my mother got me a black, handmade wooden box. She told me it was to help me save some of my money. With every dollar that I'd make from working across the street at my neighbor's horse stalls or at my friend's dad's farm, I'd come home and give whatever I had left (after paying for a soda or dirt-bike fuel) to my mom. She'd put it inside the box.

When I wanted something new—a go-kart or new tires for my four-wheeler—I'd set a goal of how much I would have to save to make it a reality. If the tires were $60, I'd save $60. If I wanted to ride my dirt bike, I needed fuel; if I needed fuel, I would have to work. My mom would always let me know, "Hey Chris, you've saved enough to do that."

At sixteen, I started working in restaurants because that's what you do when you're sixteen in rural New York. I also wanted a brand new Kawasaki 125 dirt bike. It would be my first *new* bike. All summer long, I worked at Wide Waters restaurant. I gave my mom 100% of what I made, and she put it all in that little black, wooden box.

I had no idea how much money I had, and the day that Mom and I went to look at the Kawasaki 125, she surprised me by saying, "What if you could have it right now?"

I had saved enough money for my first brand-new bike. I rode that bike every single day. It was my pride and joy. I'd come home and polish it so it always looked brand-new.

Long before I ever understood what Infinite Banking was, my mother taught me the power of being my own bank—all through the power of that little black, wooden box.

Fast-forward to 2014, when my friend and lender Mike Baird and I met in Utah at the Cheesecake Factory. He told me about "this thing" that he had learned from a man named Brent Kesler. He told me that I had to meet Brent.

As I listened to Mike tell me his story, I said, "Mike, dude, I'm a financial advisor. What you're talking about has got to be life insurance." He told me that what he was talking about was whole life insurance, in particular, and that it worked differently than other insurances in its ability to produce cash flow. We went back and forth in a greater Cheesecake Factory debate, until curiosity won and I decided that I had to learn about "this thing" that sounded too good to be true.

I called Brent and told him that I was an advisor and that I knew all about this stuff.

"Hold on a second," he said. "I need you to watch a video before we can talk."

"No, no, no, you don't understand. I understand this. I don't need to watch a video."

"You have to watch my video," he said.

The video was an hour-and-a-half long. After telling Brent that I didn't know when I'd find an hour and a half to watch it, I walked into my basement that Sunday with my coffee—a big coffee—set it down, got out my notepad, and started to watch the video. An hour and a half went by so fast that it felt like fifteen minutes. At the end of the video, I had pages upon pages of notes and my coffee was barely even touched. I was so blown away by what I'd seen.

I was probably the worst possible student for Brent because I thought I understood what I didn't understand. When I saw the video, the first thing that came to my mind was: *holy crap, this exists,* and, *holy crap, I've been missing this the whole time!* I was so intrigued—and then I was overcome with a sense of anger for never having been shown this as a financial advisor.

Brent invited me out to Mexico to see an advanced training session. Lorissa and I went out for three days. I was glued to Brent's every word. Everything he said, I absorbed. All the other people in the room were already doing Infinite Banking, and I was starting to see the business aspect of it.

All I could think was, *people need to hear about this.*

At that point, Lorissa and I were doing a lot of real estate deals and were on our way to a filming for an HGTV pilot episode. A lot of things were happening in our lives. We opened our first banking policy after that trip to Mexico, and we took my old whole life policies, which I had started back in 2004 and 2005, and moved them into the system to begin banking with them as well.

That was how I climbed out of nearly $120,000 in debt, got rid of all my credit cards and lines of credit, and freed myself from all 401(k) debt. Lorissa and I immediately began taking policy loans, paying off our credit cards, and putting the money back into the banking policy. When I kept doing this, everything happened fast. I had so much recaptured money from my debt and expenses. I began giving loans to my real-estate-investing students at FlipOut Academy™ and funded new business opportunities.

Today, I have six banking policies, and every time I look at them, there is more and more money just sitting there, waiting for me to do something with it. My life is a stark contrast to that of 2014, when I was investing my money all wrong. That's why I have dedicated myself to using my personal journey to empower you to take back control of your money and build your legacies—to give you the financial knowledge that fuels your freedom. When I tell my story today, I say, "The biggest problem somebody will ever have with Infinite Banking is that eventually, you will not know how to spend all the money. You won't know where to put all the money once you change this one thing in your financial life."

For both Lorissa and I, our personal challenges and circumstances forced us to become innovative with our money, which led us to discover what we believe to be a better way to wealth for everyone. As Infinite Banking Concept™ founder R. Nelson Nash shares in his book, *Becoming Your Own Banker*, "Hardship often helps us to see things to which we are normally blind."

It may have taken a period of hardship for you to pick up this book and seek a solution that is outside of the norm, but we are glad you are here. This is a book about your money and your wealth, and the one thing you can do differently to regain financial control and live like the wealthy.

Step inside, and we'll map out the millionaire mystery together.

The Money Multiplier Method

*What if you could get all the money back for every purchase
you've ever made? What if you could create wealth
through the debts and expenses you already have?*

SEVERAL YEARS AGO, BRENT AND his wife attended a
motivational event in Kansas City. It was the kind of event
that featured the likes of Zig Ziglar, Brian Tracy, and Colin
Powell and was designed to promote positive thinking. As they
listened to the speakers, they were constantly encouraged to
do things differently and to think outside the box.

At the break, many of the nearly eight thousand people
in the arena rushed to the bathroom. There was a line for
the women's bathroom, a very long line. Brent and his wife
took one quick glance at the line and decided to find another
bathroom.

After a ninety-second walk around the corner, they found a second bathroom, located right behind the concession stand. It had twenty empty stalls. Empty.

As they walked back to their seats, they passed the long line of people at the other bathroom.

"Hey, all, walk down there ninety seconds and there's an empty bathroom. Nobody's there," Brent said.

Not a single person stepped out of line to go to the empty bathroom. Not one. Brent and his wife looked at each other, astounded. They were at a conference that promoted outside-the-box thinking and were there to "change the world," yet, not a single person moved. They were all inclined to do what everyone else was doing.

Doing One Thing Differently

We've been taught that money works in a certain way. It is costing us our financial freedom because we are doing things with our money that we'd never do with the things that money buys. If you are like most Americans, you've spent your entire adult life paying the banks, your creditors, and your expenses. At the same time, you've watched your retirement funds and legacy drastically fluctuate or evaporate in the markets.

Most of us are directing our financial focus to places or investments over which we have no control—those that are tied to the markets—because it's what we've been told to do, and *it's what everyone else is doing.* Well, everyone else isn't always right—especially when they're waiting in painfully long lines when there are empty bathroom stalls ninety seconds around the corner.

Getting out of the mud of any current financial struggle, and getting to the top of the mountain only becomes easier when you're using the right vehicle and operating it to its maximum efficiency. It all begins with thinking differently about money.

In a viral YouTube video called "The Backwards Brain Bicycle – Smarter Every Day," narrator Destin Sandlin talks about how he was taught to ride a bike when he was really young . . . though everything changed twenty-five years later when his colleague Barney called him up. The welders at his office were geniuses and liked to play jokes on the engineers. They had built Destin a special bicycle and wanted him to try to ride it.

The welders only changed one thing about the bicycle: When you turned the handlebars to the left, the bike went to the right. When you turned the handlebars to the right, the bike went to the left—the opposite of what we are used to.

Destin tried to ride the bike, and he simply could not do it. At that moment, he had a revelation: his thinking was in a rut. He had the knowledge of how to operate the bike, but he didn't have the understanding. In his own words, "Once you have a rigid way of thinking in your head, sometimes you cannot change that, even if you want to."

The good news is that we know you can change your thinking about money. Absorbing and adopting the understanding (more than just the knowledge) delivered to you in this book is going to help you do just that.

It took Destin eight months to successfully maneuver the backward bicycle. He did it by being attentive to and changing his thinking. We want to help you to do the same with money and wealth, in much less time.

Before you know it, you will be just like Destin, who said, "I can't ride a bike like you anymore," and that will be a *very* good thing—for your wealth, your family, and your legacy.

The irony of the backward bicycle is that it created forward thinking. We want to help you realize that The Money Multiplier Method, based on R. Nelson Nash's Infinite Banking Concept™, is a forward-thinking way to money management and sustainable wealth. To have true success, the one thing you need to do and think about differently is to understand that you can *control the environment in which you operate.*

Every single one of us has the power to change our financial trajectory by stepping outside of the norm and adding one simple step to our financial life: becoming our own bank. Founder of the Infinite Banking Concept™ R. Nelson Nash says, "When you own the capital, you have the control."

He also says, "There has got to be some honest introspection at this point, and a commitment to 'get out of financial prison' must be a burning passion. This is going to require a change in priorities in life and recognizing that *controlling the banking function personally is the most important thing that can be done in your financial world.*"[1]

Those who have realized the greatest financial success know that our wealth is a result of the financial habits and strategies we live by. The wealthiest people know differently than most. They use a two-hundred-year-old strategy to eliminate debt, grow their wealth, minimize taxation, and leave a legacy to their heirs. What the wealthy know and do differently all centers around the banking function—controlling the environment.

Robert Kiyosaki, Tony Robbins, and R. Nelson Nash all talk about this secret. Walt Disney used it to build Disney World. Ray Kroc used it to build the McDonald's franchise. Sears and J. C. Penney have similar founding stories. The Money Multiplier Method is founded upon this little-known but long-standing and exponentially powerful strategy used by the top 5%.

R. Nelson Nash says, "Everyone should be in two businesses—the one in which you make your living, and the other should be the banking business that finances whatever you do for a living. Of the two businesses, banking is the most important."

He defines the Infinite Banking Concept™, which he founded in the 1980s, as "an exercise in imagination, reason, logic, and prophecy. . . . It is all about recovering the interest that one normally pays to some banking institution and then lending it to others so that the policy owner makes what a banking institution does. It is like building an environment in the airplane world where you have a perpetual 'tailwind' instead of a perpetual 'headwind.'"[2]

Before reading this book, you may have thought it impossible to have control over the environment in which your investments sit . . . though with The Money Multiplier Method—the modern-day, elaborate process of creating your own banking system—you become the owner and the banker, and you have full control over how your money is used.

This is about taking responsibility for your wealth and your legacy, and not leaving it in the hands of the banks, investment companies, and government.

Inside this book is the education, understanding, and process you need to change your financial trajectory and reclaim control of your financial future. It all stems from you becoming your own banker, so that you can truly build your wealth and legacy.

We're going to teach you about a newly defined financial *mission*, unveil shocking financial *mysteries*, detail the *machine* that will change your financial destiny, and outline the *marathon* thinking and requirements that will help you become the *millionaire*. Finally, we'll talk about this *movement* and all the places it can take you when you free yourself from financial slavery and regain control of your finances to generate more money for the following:

- Retirement
- Lifestyle
- Family
- Real Estate Deals
- Legacy

You can have full control of your financial future *and* how your money is used today. It sounds too good to be true, only because most people simply don't understand how it all works. We will help you to fully understand how The Money Multiplier Method works and show you that it is, in fact, *not* too good to be true (as we both originally thought it to be). We'll give you the process to keep control and ownership of your capital because we believe that change, for the better, only happens when we are willing to speak up and speak out.

Financial educator and founder of Rich Global LLC and the Rich Dad Company, Robert Kiyosaki, also teaches the Infinite Banking Concept™ through his work. He believes in personal responsibility and in "changing the things we have the ability to change and control." In *Second Chance: for Your*

Money, Your Life and Our World—he argues that "many people need a second chance to rethink what they work for." He says, "Each of us has the power to change ourselves. And the easiest—and often most powerful—change we can make is through education."[3]

Tony Robbins, the nation's top life and business strategist, says, "Contrary to popular wisdom, knowledge is not power—it's *potential* power. Knowledge is not mastery. *Execution* is mastery."

When we think we know it all, we stop learning, yet we do not know what we've never been taught. The greatest financial knowledge is not taught, *it's sought out*. You will step into your power and into your wealth by seeking out, understanding, and executing the financial truths delivered inside this book.

Next time you think to yourself, *Should I or shouldn't I?*, we want you to remember those who refused to move from the long bathroom line and be the one who is willing to step away from where everyone else is standing—waiting for their lives (and financial trajectory) to change—and go where not many others are going. We want you to start your own line, your own legacy.

It's time to stand out by taking back the banking functions in your life and taking back control of your money. Let's get started!

The Mission

*You didn't know the truth about money
because your parents and teachers didn't know the truth.
Today things change. Today you learn how money really works.*

ARLIER THIS MONTH, BRENT WAS flying back from Greenville, South Carolina to Lake of the Ozarks in Camdenton, Missouri. It was nearly noon when he landed his plane, and John, a longtime airport attendee, greeted him at the airport.

On that particular day, John opened up a deeper conversation than they had shared during their previous encounters. He began asking Brent about his business and "the stuff that he does." When somebody asks Brent about his role, his answer is always the same. He says, "I teach people how to build wealth through their own debts and expenses that they already have." It's almost verbatim what R. Nelson Nash used to say.

"How would you like to have a way to get all the money back you've ever paid for every debt and expense you've ever had as you continue to build your wealth?" Brent asked John. "For example, John, the car that you bought. You only bought it in one of three ways. You paid cash for it, bank financed it, or you leased it, right? Because I think you're an honest guy, and you didn't steal the car. You had to give money to the car dealer, the car dealer gave you the car, and everybody walked away happy. The transaction was done. But what if I could show you a way to not only get the car, to buy it exactly the way that you did, but also get all of the money back that you paid for the car?"

John said that he wished he had known Brent earlier so he could have helped him with his money. He was in his seventies and trying to find his way back to retirement after financial hardship. A few years back, he was living in Olathe, Kansas, and had retired after years of military service. He and his wife had $400,000 at the time—and they surrendered it all to the local "investment guy."

There was a room at the bank where John had been banking for years; it was where people went to see this investment guy.

He had decided to go in because his friends who banked with the same bank did it, his neighbors did it, the guy he played cards with did it, and the guy he walked his dog with did it. He figured that if everyone else was doing it, it *had* to be good. Since he wasn't overly financially savvy, he went with the crowd and did what everyone else was doing.

"I went in the room, and before I knew it, I'd given complete control of my $400,000 to the banker. I didn't really look into it. And when I didn't hear from him for a while, I just figured everything was going good. Then, all of a sudden, I got a call one day. It was the investment guy. He said, 'Hey, John, I've got some bad news for you. All of your money is gone.'"

When John asked the banker where his money was, the only answer he got was, "It's complicated." Everything John owned was gone, and the bank was no longer in business.

Brent's stomach turned as he sat with John. He wanted to know more, but didn't want to pry. Meeting John made Brent think about what we do and how we sometimes don't really think about our money. We don't question handing over full control to somebody else simply because they have on a suit and tie, look and smell good, and all of our neighbors are dealing with them.

As a society, we've been taught to put our money into stocks, bonds, mutual funds, qualified plans, IRAs, and 401(k)s. In other words, we're told to give away the control of our money to someone else, to let them play around with it.

We figure that it's going to be OK . . . until it isn't.

We've also been told that we have to go to school, study hard, get good grades, and turn our future over to a company or be willing to start at the bottom and work our way up.

In *MONEY Master the Game: 7 Simple Steps to Financial Freedom*—a book committed to setting people up so they have an income for life without ever having to work again—Tony Robbins says, "We're not about to *earn* our way to wealth. That's a mistake millions of Americans make. We think that if we work harder, smarter, longer, we'll achieve our financial dreams, but our paycheck alone—no matter how big—isn't the answer."

Many of you have worked incredibly hard, paid your fair share to the government, put your money in the banks, and moved throughout life, yet you're nowhere near where you want to be financially. You've attempted to do what your wealthier neighbors have done, and you aren't even close to being financially free.

For too long, we've been giving up control of our finances and unnecessarily assuming additional risk. In order to move into becoming our own bank and living like the wealthy, we need to begin by changing two things: how we think about money and how we approach our spending (and saving).

An Obsession with Spending

At the end of the fiscal year 2018, the total federal debt in the United States was $21.6 trillion.[4] That's the highest the debt has ever been. We're obsessed with spending and living for today. We are driven by the survivalist thinking of keeping up with a society that wants the best of everything at every moment, and we, as North Americans, are statistically not focused on the big picture of what we truly need for today and tomorrow.

In the 1990s, Infinite Banking Concept™ founder R. Nelson Nash studied the spending habits of American families. He maintained a close watch on the income allocated to automobiles, housing, living, and saving. At the time of the publication of *Becoming Your Own Banker*, Nash addressed spending habits, saying that in relation to the proportion of income allocated to each category, "This seems to be the current situation, which doesn't seem to change all that much."

What Nash discovered then still applies today. He built his Infinite Banking scenarios around "the All-American family" because he didn't want people to think that you have to be rich to create a banking system that can handle all your financial needs.[5]

He determined that in the average American household:

- Twenty cents of every dollar goes toward automobiles— the cost of the car and the maintenance.

- Thirty cents of every dollar goes toward housing.

- Forty cents of every dollar goes toward everything else in life, including travel, food, and charitable giving.

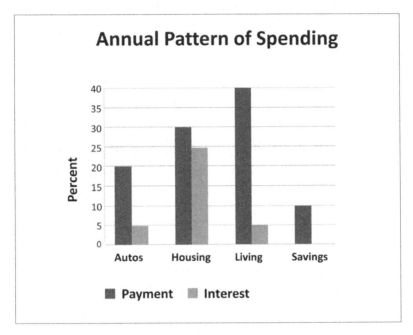

We're spending and giving away to others ninety cents on every dollar. In September 2019, the current average savings rate in North America was 8.3%.[6]

Our greatest financial struggles stem from focusing on working for our money instead of having our money work for us. Add in our propensity to spend far more than we save without maximizing the wealth-building capacity of our spending, and that is how we've found ourselves where we are today.

When financial advisors talk to you about your money, they are talking to you about what you are *saving*—and in order to save more, you believe that you have to take on more risk and have less of what you want and need for your business and your lifestyle. The Money Multiplier Method is different because **we're going to focus on the money you are spending**. If we can take some of the money that you are already spending and move (or transfer) it into your savings, we've increased your savings rate, and we've done so without working any harder, without assuming additional risk, without losing control of your money, and without changing your cash flow.

The Money Multiplier Method of Infinite Banking is a truly unique financial machine because it allows you to manage and maximize your wealth, as you live and spend as you typically do . . . versus halting your spending to save your money in a retirement vehicle (where you have no access to your money for many years). While both can be used in tandem, it's important to distinguish the two. A retirement vehicle is not going to empower you to recapture all of the money you've spent on every car you've ever owned, ever. *We* are.

Before we get into the workings of The Money Multiplier Method, it's important to understand how money works, uncover the illusions of retirement freedom, and investigate the mysteries of the third-party banking functions that we've all become accustomed to.

How Money Really Works

Everything we want to create in our business and personal lives begins with money. Renowned American businessman and author Zig Ziglar put it best when he said, "Money isn't everything, but, it's reasonably close to oxygen on the 'gotta have it' scale."

The world is full of plans, gurus, and clutter that keep us in the dark about our money. It doesn't help that we have been unintentionally misled to think that money is bad or that we're too dumb to understand how to make, save, and spend it (i.e., that we need to pay and trust someone else to do so for us).

The whole conversation in this book is about money— how money flows, what money does, and what you do with money—because what you don't know *is* hurting you. Global financial educator Robert Kiyosaki says, "The big shift must come in education, not only in what we teach, but how we teach." Let's talk about what money is and how it really works.

Simply put, money is just a means of exchange for goods and services. In other words, we exchange money for food, food for money, money for cars, cars for money, money for houses, houses for money, money for vacations, and vacations for money.

Tony Robbins says, "At its core, money is about power. We've all seen how money can have the power to create or the power to destroy."[7] He goes on to say, "One thing is for sure: you either use it, or it uses you."[8]

In his book, *Second Chance: for Your Money, Your Life and Our World*, Robert Kiyosaki says that measuring wealth in money will cause "the rich to become the new poor."[9]

He points out several reasons:

1. Because "money is no longer money."

2. Because "knowledge is the new money."

3. Because the poor and middle class of today have the opportunity to "become the new rich of tomorrow."

Elaborating on his belief that money will cause "the rich to become the new poor," Kiyosaki makes the bold statement that "our wealth is stolen via our money."

He points out three areas where our money is disappearing:

1. **Taxes** – The value of our labor is stolen through taxes.

2. **Inflation** – Prices increase when the government prints money.

3. **Savings** – As Kiyosaki says, "Savers are losers" because banks steal savers' wealth via the "fractional reserve system" banking process (a form of printing money).

If knowledge is the new money, and execution is true power, this book is going to give you the power to reclaim control of your money—your income-producing and wealth-building power—so that you can live the lifestyle you want, have the retirement you want, and leave the legacy you want.

Illusions of Retirement Freedom

Thirty-four million baby boomers are currently in retirement.[10] The remainder of the seventy million baby boomers are getting ready to retire,[11] and almost half of Americans approaching retirement have little to nothing saved.[12] When we do have something saved, and we put our money away into retirement accounts, we give away our money (and our power) to those who are willing to handle these accounts for us. The trouble is that we don't know if they've done a good job until it may be too late, like John, an airport employee, who trusted "the investment guy" all of his friends and neighbors used, only to lose all of his $400,000 retirement fund.

What do we really know about our retirement accounts? You likely know if the money goes up or down, based on the quarterly statements you get. You also may know whether your money is invested in a low-, moderate-, or high-risk category. Other than that, most people don't know *shit* about what their money is doing.

In his book, *MONEY Master the Game*, Tony Robbins states that "Polls show that fewer than one in four trust the financial system—with good reason!"[13]

Robert Kiyosaki says, "Today, millions of Americans, through their 401(k)s and IRAs, blindly turn their money over to people they do not know or trust. They follow the instructions of parrots, repeating what they have been told to say. That's a risky proposition."[14]

When you put your money into these government-sponsored accounts, you put all of your trust and all of your money into someone else's hands without any guarantee as to what will happen to your funds within the accounts. There is no protection of your funds if "Wall Street sinks into the New York Harbor," as R. Nelson Nash said. "The most dangerous thing you can do with money is put it into government-sponsored schemes," he concluded.

While his words may seem harsh, it is critical to consider both the risk you are taking in the markets and with your "investment guy (or gal)" *and* how much you are *actually* earning within those accounts.

Are you buying into an average return, and how does it compare to your actual return? Take, for instance, a man we'll call Robert Dolitte. Robert was recommended to an investment advisor by his brother. Given that the advisor came highly recommended, dressed nicely, and drove a nice car, Robert trusted him. When Robert was told that this advisor's clients "earned an average 25% return on their investments," he bought in. The trouble was that after four years, Robert realized a whopping return rate of 0%. Why? Because of the difference between average and actual returns.

Ready for the Math Lesson?

Average *Actual*

Year	Starting Investment	Ending Investment	Return
1	$100	$200	+100%
2	$200	$100	−50%
3	$100	$200	+100%
4	$200	$100	−50%

The financial advisor was, in fact, telling the truth: the average rate of return over four years was 25%:

$$[(-50\%) + 100\% + (-50\%) + 100\%] / 4 = 25\%$$

When Robert was invited out to a celebratory dinner sponsored by his advisor's office, the celebration was short-lived because he looked inside his account and saw that all he had was the money he had started with, less the management fees and taxes. On top of that, his $100 in year four were weaker dollars; they were worth less than the $100 he'd started with in year one.

All this is to say that it is critical to focus on your actual rate of return when considering where to put your money, which is what we do in The Money Multiplier Method.

If giving up control of your finances and being marketed unrealistic "average return" rates on your traditional investments isn't painful enough, when you invest in retirement accounts, you're also giving away your good dollars today in exchange for weaker dollars later.

When you put your money away into 401(k)s and IRAs, you do so with the intention of getting your money *later*—years down the road. You have to lock your money away for years before you can use it. You cannot get to your money without paying penalties and taxes, until you turn 59½. The reality is that if you are contributing to a 401(k), an IRA, or another qualified plan, you might as well forget about your money since you can't touch it today or tomorrow. The saying, "Out of sight, out of mind" holds very true.

You also give up the opportunity to use your money today, while the value of the dollar is still strong. This means you are faced with the opportunity cost of not being able to put the money toward your house, your car, your business, or your lifestyle.

Here's a critical question: Is a dollar worth more today or in the future?

The answer is *today*. You could buy more candy bars twenty years ago for $1 than you can today.

If you go to the grocery store today and buy milk, a steak, and a loaf of bread, would you wait twenty years to drink that milk and eat that steak and bread? Of course not. This is the source of our pain and struggle around money and what we've been taught to believe.

When you put money in a government- or employer-sponsored retirement plan—a 401(k), an IRA, or another qualified plan—what you're doing is buying a loaf of bread and putting it in the freezer. In, say, twenty years, you open the freezer and see two loaves of bread (representing the growth of your money). Is that second loaf of bread any good? No, it's still freezer burned! Tomorrow's dollars will never be worth as much as today's.

Robert Kiyosaki explains this by saying, "The opposite of saving is known as the 'velocity of money.' Most people 'park' their money where they save or invest for retirement. Smart people keep their money moving. Simply put, when you park your money, your money loses value. When you keep your money moving, your money increases in value."[15]

The second critical question is this: Are taxes going to go up or down?

Taxes, like most everything else, go up, and even if they don't go up, you will be taxed on more goods (of greater cost) than you were in the past. Robert Kiyosaki says, "Inflation is good for debtors and bad for savers, which is why savers are losers."[16]

The third critical question is as follows: Would you rather pay taxes on the seed or on the harvest? In other words, do you want to pay tax on the money you invest (the small amount) or the money you make (the large amount)?

The small amount, right?

When you invest in retirement plans, you are violating your own desires because you are being taxed on your harvest (the large future amount). When you take the money out, taxation is going to occur on that money. The only thing you're avoiding by taking your money out at the proper age is the penalty.

We've been taught to give away our good dollars today and get paid back with weaker dollars in the future. The Money Multiplier Method is totally contradictive to the conventional way of thinking about money, as we are focusing on *using* **our good dollars today and** *paying back* **others with weaker dollars in the future,** *and,* **as we mentioned earlier, we are going to focus on the money you are spending, rather than solely the money you are saving**.

By having and being your own banking system, versus relying solely on traditional investment methods, you no longer have to lock up your cash, you no longer have to turn over control to someone else, you can continue to spend for your lifestyle and business, and you can realize growth guarantees from day one.

R. Nelson Nash says, "There are only two sources of income—people at work and money at work." You can either continue to work hard and turn your hard-earned dollars over to someone else to control, or you can make the choice to think differently, become your own bank, and make your money work for you.

It's time to choose to be in control of your money from the beginning and every day thereafter. The Money Multiplier Method is built upon three foundational principles for your life and your money:

1. **Pay Yourself First.** We think we know it, but it can be hard to do. It's easy to give away our money to the car people, the house people, the TV people, the electricity people, the grocery people, the school people, the investment guy. It's time to keep your money before giving it away.

2. **Pay Yourself with Interest.** Millionaires understand that there is a premium and privilege put on using their money. With The Money Multiplier Method, you're going to learn to treat your money just as you would the bank's money. When you borrow money, you pay it back with interest. If money flows out of your banking systems, money should be put back in to replace it.

3. **Recapture What You Spend.** Recapturing and recycling the money you spend is one of the most powerful processes you'll ever learn. You can get back all of the

money you spend on cars, your home, and even your charitable giving and taxes, all the while building your wealth and legacy. That's what The Money Multiplier Method is about!

In order to become your own bank, recycle and recapture the interest you're paying out to everyone else, and regain full control of your finances, we need to investigate the system itself—how banks really work and what we can learn from them.

Get ready to unlock the mysteries!

The Mysteries

*Until you understand the truth of how banks work,
you cannot begin to think like them and implement
the strategies that lead you to live like the wealthy.*

WHEN YOU THINK OF MILLIONAIRES, you often think of who they are today without questioning how they got to where they are. Most people can't think of what came before Disneyland and Disney World, or how they came to be. It's easy to assume that things came easily to Walt Disney, and the money just flowed.

> *"It takes a lot of money to make these dreams come true.
> From the very start it was a problem. Getting the money
> to open Disneyland. About $17 million it took. And we had
> everything mortgaged, including my personal insurance."*
> **—Walt Disney**

There's an important lesson to be revealed when we dive into the rich history that belongs to Walt Disney and his empire—an empire that wasn't always so magical.

Disney began his career with the Kansas City Film Ad Company in Missouri in 1920. In 1922, he and his friend, animator Ub Iwerks, founded the Laugh-O-Gram Studio in Kansas City and began producing cartoons based on fables and fairy tales.

Disney started his movie company with only $750 in funding. Seeking a business loan, he visited conventional banks. Unsurprisingly, he was turned down and was forced to look elsewhere for funding or face the dreaded reality of giving up on his dream.

In 1953, he realized he needed a creative solution and started thinking outside the box. He discovered he could take a loan from his life insurance policy with New York Life to get the funds he needed to start his company.

His little movie company eventually blossomed into what is better known as Disneyland and Disney World, and the Walt Disney Company now has annual revenues of over $59 billion.

Walt Disney isn't the only famous person to implement the two-hundred-year-old concept of using whole life insurance policies to fund debt and expenses and generate wealth. Joe Biden, Ray Kroc (McDonald's), and Leland Stanford (Stanford University) are just a few more individuals who saw a prosperous future by using The Money Multiplier Method and Infinite Banking Concept™ strategies. The wealthiest families of our era—the Rothschilds, Morgans, Stanleys, Barkleys, and Rockefellers—all implemented similar strategies to create their wealth. They are the same strategies that Brent used to get rid of nearly $1 million in third-party consumer debt in just over three years. They all used Infinite Banking and understood how money and banking really work.

Why do the rich seem to get richer without having to work any harder? Robert Kiyosaki speaks to two reasons why so many among us are suffering and failing to step into the secrets that allow us to live like the wealthy: "Millions of people are poor or struggle financially simply because they use 'poor' or incorrect words. Millions of people struggle financially because they refer to their 'liabilities' as 'assets.'"

Robert says, "It's possible that the two most important words in the world of money are *cash* and *flow*. Cash flow determines whether something is an asset or a liability. If you understand the meaning of the words *cash flow*, *asset*, and *liability*, your chances for a richer life are greatly improved. The reason most people struggle financially is because they have lots of cash flowing out—and very little flowing in."[17]

"Assets put money in [your] pocket. Liabilities take money from [your] pocket," he says as he explains that cash flow distinguishes assets from liabilities. He also states that our wealth is *based on cash flow*, not net worth.

We're going to focus on both of the sources of struggle that Kiyosaki mentions. As we show you how banks really work—and the strategies that they can teach you—the discussion is centered around understanding what creates cash flow. In order to become the bank, you need to think like the bank (and use the right words) and focus on cash flow.

How Banks Really Work

Say you have $100,000. What do you do with your money? You take it and deposit it into the bank. For example purposes, say that you've found a really, really good bank account that pays you 4% interest. When you put money into the bank, that money becomes a liability to the bank, because they owe you interest. (Remember that anything that depletes cash flow is a liability.) The bank then takes your money and turns it into an asset by loaning it out to others. (Loans are assets to banks because they make banks money; they create cash flow.)

Banks are in the money business—the lending business. The money you put into your bank account gets loaned back to you or out to someone else to buy a house, a car, etc. The banks bring money in and move it out continuously—keeping the money in motion, and they do so in a way that is favorable to them from a cash-flow perspective.

If you are earning that aforementioned 4% on the money in your account, and your bank is loaning out that money to you (or someone else) at an interest rate of 7%, you (or that someone else) are expected to pay the bank back the full amount of the loan, plus the 7% interest.* The bank is in full control of the transaction and benefits through the creation of the loan—the asset.

Regardless of what you want to borrow money for—a car, house remodeling, a new deck, a swimming pool, a boat—you are expected to pay back the loan plus interest. Therefore, if you take a loan at 8% to buy a car, you have to pay back the full amount of the loan, plus the 8% interest. If you want to get a home equity line, borrowing money from the bank at say 9%, you pay back the amount of your loan, plus the 9% interest.* If you want to take out a debt consolidation loan at, say, 12% and use it to pay off all your credit cards, you pay off all your credit cards and then the loan has to be paid back to the bank, plus the 12% interest. Money is always going back into the banking system, and the bank is in control, as they are continuously moving money in and out.

What if we told you that through this process, the bank made 500% more than you did with the 4% interest you were earning on the money you have placed in the bank account? Let's look at the math:

- If you are earning 4% and the bank is lending it out to you or someone else as a homebuyer at 7%, the bank is making 3% more.
- If you are earning 4% and the bank is lending it out to you or someone else to buy a car at 8%, the bank is making 4% more.

How Banks Works

- If you are earning 4% and the bank is lending it out to you or someone else to do a home remodel at 9%, the bank is making 5% more.

- If you are earning 4% and the bank is lending it out to you or someone else to consolidate debt at 12%, the bank is making 8% more.

- 3% + 4% + 5% + 8% = 20% . . . that's 20% more than you, but there's more to this equation. If you make $4 on every $100 and the bank makes $20, they make five times, or 500%, more than you!

On almost any downtown corner of every town, large and small, you are bound to see a bank. Their buildings are typically the nicest buildings in town. By putting money into your bank accounts and taking out bank loans, you are paying for those buildings. The bank is in control of your money, and they are taking very little risk in using *your* money to loan out to others. To further protect themselves, the higher risk you are, the higher the interest rate you are going to have to pay, and if you are too high a risk, the banks simply won't lend to you.

Banks are making between 400% and 1,300% on the money you put in and leave there each and every year. The annual reports of banks will show you how much they are making on the money you have there. Rarely, if ever, has this number been below 400%.[20]

The Power of a Decreasing Balance

When Chris got his first new car—a Chevy S10 ZR2 pickup— he was in his late teens and running his Phatman Boardshop stores. Leasing that car was his biggest accomplishment at the time—a time when he worked tremendously hard for every dollar that went into his little black box. His payment was $175 a month, the equivalent of what he paid himself each week (as a teenage CEO in the late 1990s). Even though he had all these clothing stores, Chris was still living at home with his mom. It was hard for him to get ahead when the car company controlled his lease payments, much like it is for any of us who have the bank controlling our loan repayments and interest payments.

What happens when you finance a car or other purchase? Infinite Banking Concept™ founder R. Nelson Nash puts it very simply:

1. You pay interest to another party, or
2. You give up interest you could have earned.

He says, "You 'FINANCE' everything you buy. You either pay interest to someone else, or you give up interest you could have earned elsewhere. There are no exceptions." The latter is called "opportunity cost"—money that you could have potentially earned interest on. The solution is to create a process, a system, that you own and control the environment—one in which you make money on your loans. We call this process The Money Multiplier Method, using specifically designed whole life insurance policies as the banking system.

Even for those of you who are good with money and pay cash for your cars, you are not outside of having to make payments. By paying cash for your car, you're simply making *one large* payment up front, versus making monthly payments over several years. Paying cash for your car also does not keep you from paying interest. There is still an opportunity cost. The $25,000 you paid for the car goes to the car dealer (money is a means of exchange), and you have given up the interest you could have earned on that $25,000 if it were in your bank.

Say you want to buy a car for $25,000. Let's assume that this is precisely the amount you have in your bank account—the one we talked about in the last example that is paying you a generous 4% interest. You ask to take $25,000 of your money from the bank to pay cash for your car, but instead, your banker uses your account as collateral and gives you a 6% loan for the $25,000. You go along with it.

Based on what we taught you about how banks work, you now know that the bank will make more on the 6% interest from the loan they gave you than you will on your 4% interest-bearing bank account. What if we also told you that your banker actually *did right by you* by wanting to give you a 6% loan rather than have you take out the $25,000 in cash from your 4% interest-bearing account?

It's true. Let's look at the math:

- Your loan costs you $28,999 over sixty months ($25,000 loan + the 6% interest).

- In the meantime, the $25,000 you had in the 4% bank account has grown to $30,525 over the same sixty-month period.

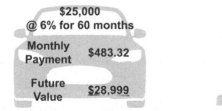
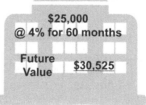

YOU'VE MADE: $1,526

The reason you were better off taking the $25,000 loan at 6% and leaving your money in the bank is because the interest charged on the money the bank loaned you is simple interest, paid on a *decreasing balance* (you are paying back the $25,000 loan over time, therefore decreasing the balance upon which interest is charged). The interest on your bank account is on an *increasing balance* (you are earning uninterrupted compound interest, which is increasing the balance in your account).

Our minds are not programmed to think that we can *make money* by paying 6% (simple) interest while earning only 4% (compound) interest. We think that if we borrow at 6% and earn at 4%, we're not making money, but that's not how money works. You can make money all day long by paying 6% and earning 4% with The Money Multiplier Method.

Regarding loans, the Federal Reserve Bank of New York says that there were over a million more "troubled borrowers" at the end of 2018 than there were in 2010.[21] Times have changed, but our need for a new strategy has not. The way we think about money needs to change.

Too often, we also get hung up on the rate of interest we are paying without giving due attention to the *amount* of interest we are paying. For instance, look at your mortgage statement within the first seven years of your thirty-year mortgage. It is likely that there is over 80% or more of your total house payment going toward interest.

The average person stays in a house for five to seven years before he or she resells or refinances it (to attain a better interest rate and term). If you have a mortgage and it is at a 5% interest rate, and your mortgage payment remains the same each month, the interest you are paying is always going to be much more than 5% because you are not able to maximize the power of a decreasing balance with 80% of your house payment going to interest in the first seven years. The principal amount is not being paid down much in the early years.

For those of you who have been in your home for over twenty years, you may have refinanced a few times. Say you have refinanced your home twice. That makes for a total of three transactions of buying and refinancing. It's not the rate of interest that is killing us, it's the volume of interest we are paying! We talk about how high of a rate of return (interest) we can get on our savings held by the banks while continuing to pay out roughly 34.5 cents on every disposable dollar as interest.[22]

We are trying to get you to think about what is really going on with your money! Banks are very smart. When you start to think more like them, you move beyond the habits of the average American household and step into the secrets of the wealthy.

Compounding Is Often Misunderstood

Do you believe in compound interest? The only way compound interest works is if your money is sitting still—remaining in the same place. If you remove your money from the bank, it no longer earns compound interest.

Motion is a natural law of the universe. You wouldn't want to eat a fish you caught out of a stagnant pond, would you? When we think of one business that uses compound interest, the most common answer is banks. In all actuality, banks do *not* use compound interest themselves. They *pay you* compound interest and *charge you* compound interest, though *they do not use it themselves.*

Say you make a large mark with a yellow highlighter on a $20 bill, initial it, and take it down to the bank. If you return to the bank in a month to retrieve that same $20 bill, you will not get it back. The bank has not kept your money in a special (little black) box for you. You will not ever be able to retrieve that particular $20 bill—not in a day, not in a week, not in a month. Why? Because as we mentioned earlier, banks are in the business of lending money, and because of this, they keep their money in motion.

No real businesses in the world actually have money sitting still to build compound interest. If a car dealer doesn't move cars, they don't make money. If a grocery store doesn't move the products off their shelves, they don't make money. All the institutions that promote compound interest—banks, Wall Street, mutual funds, and insurance companies—tell us to park our money with them, but they don't park the money themselves! They keep it in motion, using it to earn interest (*cash flow*) for themselves.

In the financial world, we continually hear about how good compound interest is. If this is the case, why aren't these larger institutions using it? It all comes down to *how* we use uninterrupted compound interest to create our wealth.

In his book, *MONEY Master the Game*, Tony Robbins speaks of his interview with Burton Malkiel, the man behind index funds. When Robbins asked Malkiel, "What's the biggest misstep most of us make right from the start?" Malkiel said, "The majority of investors fail to take full advantage of the incredible power of compounding—the multiplying power of growth times growth."[23]

The money you put into your whole life insurance policy is put to work by the insurance company, so they are ensuring the compounding benefits on the growth of your policy value. At the same time, you get to act much like the banks and keep your money in motion—by taking out loans from the general fund of the insurance company. More on that in the next chapter.

In the upcoming chapters, we are going to show you how to pay off debt and recapture the interest you are paying to everyone else, including how to get back all of your money for every car you will ever buy, drive, and own . . . because today, *everything changes*.

Today, *you* become the bank. Today, you pay yourself first. The solution to breaking free from the bonds of financial slavery and living like the wealthy is that simple.

The Machine

How you use the machine to build your wealth and replicate the secrets that the wealthy already know is what determines your capacity to live like them.

DAVE ULLOA GREW UP HAVING everything he needed, but not everything he wanted. He was born in New York and raised in a humble family. His father was a deli man from Ecuador, and his mom was a cleaning lady from El Salvador. As a child, Dave would get his brother's hand-me-downs, even if they were too small. He longed for things that were nicer and wanted the best things in life, to be successful, and to make money.

After earning his college degree in criminal justice, Dave became a police officer with the Los Angeles Police Department.

The job wasn't about making money for him, so when the money coming in didn't keep pace with his desire for the nicer things in life, things got tough. Dave loved BMWs, so he got one. He also got a Maserati because he believed in getting his dream cars. He and his wife racked up $70,000 in credit card debt and were living paycheck to paycheck—with two very nice cars sitting in the driveway.

Dave had not been able to master the secrets of the wealthy until one day when he and his wife went to visit her college friend for dinner. This friend had married an investment banker and lived in a stunning home in the Hollywood Hills. Dave was immediately fascinated by how this guy, who was about his age, had figured out the money game. Dave quickly learned that in order to build wealth, he had to think differently—like a millionaire.

Dave wanted to get out of the "rat race," to live in a nice house, and to be able to travel the world with his wife. After reading well over one hundred books on money, wealth, and finance, attending countless seminars and trainings, and learning from some of the best financial minds of our times, he learned many money rules that just aren't taught in school or in society. He had also expanded his network five years prior on a quest to learn the hidden truths about how the money game works. That's when he'd met Brent.

In 2015, Dave Ulloa became his own bank. He created and took loans from his whole life insurance policy. He put

10% of his money into the policy and dubbed it "The Bank of Ulloa." He began thinking like a bank (one that gives loans and makes interest) and not like a consumer (one that gets loans and pays interest).

He loaned the money for a new $79,000 BMW X5 to his corporation and charged the corporation 10% interest on the loan for sixty months. He and his wife paid cash for the car and drove it off the lot. Dave gave his corporation ownership of the car and paid the loan back to "The Bank of Ulloa" over five years—at a rate of $1,680 every month.

Over the course of the five years, the Bank of Ulloa earned $21,799.89 in interest from his corporation (which his corporation wrote off as an expense). On top of that, the $79,000 he had taken as a loan did not affect the policy value that continued to grow, earning uninterrupted compound interest over the five years.

He and his wife made money on the BWM *and* sold it for $32,000 several years later. They were also able to give the car buyers a loan at a rate of 4% interest over forty-eight months. The interest earned went right back into their banking system.

Instead of paying the banks and other people, Dave learned to pay himself. He began to use the banking system for his home and other expenses and he paid off his credit card debt. Today, he is able to get a loan for *anything* he wants—a stark contrast from the life he knew growing up.

When asked what the number one thing Dave and his wife learned in going from broke to being known as "the blue-collar millionaires," he says it is the importance of "building your financial IQ." He believes that it takes one skill set to *make* a lot of money and takes a different skill set to *keep* a lot of money.

Dave credits their financial success to five criteria:

1. Taking full control of where he put his money (i.e., not giving it away to a financial advisor to invest it for him).

2. Having low to no risk in his financial tools.

2. Having his money grow above inflation (not so safe and secure that you are hanging out in a savings account).

3. Being able to access his money in thirty days or less.

4. Investing in something that is for the greater good.

In his words, "Most people don't know the rules to the money game and therefore never win it. This is one simple process that anyone can do to begin winning at the money game. Yes, you can turn your depreciating liability of a car into an asset."

Reclaiming Control

R. Nelson Nash says, "People have abdicated their responsibility/opportunity of building their own Warehouse of Wealth and have turned the function over to the bankers. And the bankers have made them slaves!"[24]

If you're a business owner, one of the most important relationships you have is with your banker(s) because they control your finances. Successful entrepreneurs have great banking relationships. What if you could become that banker—your own banker—and reduce the risk in that relationship, all the while assuming greater control of your finances?

Banking is one of the most powerful systems in the world. It represents the way for which items are paid—the financing of a purchase. By controlling this one link in your financial system, you would be as powerful as the banking industry that surrounds us.

R. Nelson Nash says, "If you know what's really happening, you'll know what to do."

For far too long, you've been paying the banks and others a lot of interest to fund your business or pay for personal debts. Now, we turn the tables. By owning the bank, financing purchases, loaning money to yourself and others, and controlling the flow of money in your life, you will find the financial freedom you desire, just as Dave Ulloa did.

When Infinite Banking Concept™ founder, R. Nelson Nash, first bought himself a whole life policy in the late 1950s, he had no idea what he had gotten himself into. Unbeknownst to him, he had unwittingly begun a banking system that would bless his household, his family, and all of us forever.

Nash was a forestry consultant for ten years. He studied finance and dealt with compound interest for a long time, witnessing what happened when there was no taxation on growing money. After his forestry endeavors, he went on to have a thirty-year career in insurance sales. He lectured on the subject of life insurance for twelve years, and he knew how dividend-paying life insurance worked. Nash also studied and immersed himself in real estate his entire life. In the 1970s, he got into real estate development.

In November 1980, when interest rates were over 20%, his home was burglarized, his fifty-two-year-old brother dropped dead from a heart attack, his granddaughter was diagnosed with cancer at six weeks of age, and he owed $500,000 in third-party debt. When telling the story of how the Infinite Banking Concept™ was created, he says that it was "born over a period of many, many months at 3:00 a.m. to 4:00 a.m. in the kneeling position, praying, 'Lord, please show me a way out of this financial nightmare that I have created for myself.'"

Can you relate to Nash's pain? Have you felt the same at one point or another in your life—especially if you are a professional, an entrepreneur, or a real estate investor who has made (and potentially lost) significant investments in your business?

Nash's eyes were opened to see things that most people have misunderstood, and because of that, he has been able to help us all be in a position of control when it comes to managing our family money for generations.

The Money Multiplier Method is not a high-risk new market strategy, but rather, a process using a two-hundred-year-old vehicle known as dividend-paying whole life insurance to become your own bank. It is the same vehicle upon which Nash founded the Infinite Banking Concept™.

Most people think of leaving a legacy through a life insurance death benefit, but they don't realize the cash flow potential these policies have. Whole life insurance is the most fundamental vehicle that the wealthiest people and institutions have used for generations to keep their money in their families. In The Money Multiplier Method, we use a specially designed, high-premium, dividend-paying whole life insurance as the machine that powers our personally owned banking system because it allows *you* to be the 100% owner of each policy you take out. This means that you have control over where 100% of the equity of the contract is loaned out and how big the policy (cash value and death benefit) grows over time.

There are three major aspects to your ability to reclaim control of your finances by becoming your own bank and creating your banking system:

1. **You don't have to lock up your money.** If you are contributing to a government qualified plan, you need to lock your money up before you can touch it at age 59½. With your specifically designed, high-cash-value (SD, HCV) whole life policy as your banking system,

you have access to loans immediately, within the first thirty days of starting your contract.

2. **More return doesn't equal more risk.** We typically associate greater return with greater risk, but that is not the case when you use a SD, HCV whole life insurance policy as your banking system.

3. **You have guarantees.** Regardless of what happens in the financial markets, your money is guaranteed to increase in value inside your SD, HCV whole life policy.

Let's look at how all of these pieces come together when you choose to become your own bank and set up your banking system through a SD, HCV, dividend-paying whole life insurance policy.

Understanding the Machine

Life insurance, at its core, is a protection against a loss of life. You are paying an insurance company to pay to cover your loss, should it occur. They assess the damage and pay out the benefit according to how the policy was initially set up. There are two major types of life insurance: permanent and nonpermanent.

- **Nonpermanent Insurance**, or **Term Insurance**, has a start date and an end date. A typical term is up to thirty years. If you, the insured, died during the term where you are paying premiums, the company will pay out to your beneficiaries.

The bad news is that most term policies will often never pay out, because death during the term will, in most cases, be a premature death. It's like renting a house; as long as the renter is paying rent for the use of house, all rights and privileges are theirs. When the lease is up, they have no claim on the property going forward.

- **Permanent Insurance** or ordinary insurance, better known as **Whole Life Insurance**, is good for the insured's whole life. When you enter into a contract with the insurance company, they have to pay out the claim at some point. The bad news is that point involves your "graduation," as we like to say.

  Whole life insurance is like buying and owning a house; you put some of the money down and move in, even though you continue to pay toward the principal. You have equity, which means that you have money you can leverage. That money is known as cash value. The cash value is guaranteed to ultimately reach the face amount of the policy by the time the insured is between 100 and 121 years of age.

Whole life insurance policies include the following features:

1. **A Death Benefit** — Whether we want it or not, we will have a death benefit to pass on to others after we

"graduate." If three people are all in different health, but are each ten years apart (twenty-six, thirty-six, forty-six), their premiums (deposits) will vary. If they all put $10,000 deposits into their policy, the younger one will have the largest death benefit and the older one will have the smallest death benefit. They will all have the same cash value in their banking policy.

2. **Premium Deposits** — To keep our policy, we will be required to make regular deposits. Most people think of premiums as the payment, but when we are putting money into a whole life insurance policy for use as our banking system, we need to start thinking about our premiums as our *deposits*.

   Premiums go into your policy and form a large pool of money (from the number of people participating in policies with that mutual life insurance company) in order to pay out the agreed-upon death benefits. When you take a loan from your policy, it comes from this pool.

   Each year, at your policy contract renewal, the insurance company will send you a premium-deposit notice. You can automate your premium deposits by automatic draft setup and pay monthly or quarterly.

3. **Dividends** — Dividends are a bonus paid to you by the insurance company through which you've purchased your whole life policy. They are a return of unearned

(surplus) premium that has been collected by the mutual company. In other words, when insurance companies over-collect premiums, they pay out in dividends that can be taken in one of four forms. First, you can take the dividends as a check, which is taxable income. This does limit the cash benefit you can build and does not increase your death benefit as much. Second, you can elect to have your dividend payments go toward your premium, meaning you pay less out of pocket for your premiums. Third, dividends can be placed into a second interest-bearing account with a rate of growth set by the insurance company. There is no option to contribute extra to these accounts, and once you take the money out, it cannot be put back in. Fourth, your dividends can be used to purchase additional insurance, which leads to the creation of greater cash value. This is known as **paid-up additions** ("additional paid-up insurance") and also increases the death benefit.

In The Money Multiplier Method, we want to focus on what whole life insurance can do for us while we're *alive*, versus its benefits to our beneficiaries once we've "graduated." The biggest piece of the equation is our ability to take out policy loans to pay for our expenses and pay off our debts. As R. Nelson Nash says in *Becoming Your Own Banker*, "Your need for finance during your lifetime is much greater than your need for protection. Solve this need through [whole life insurance], and you will end up with more life insurance than the companies will issue on you."

Choosing the right insurance company is also critical, given our focus on achieving cash flow from the policies. At The Money Multiplier, we consider four factors when choosing our companies:

1. **Mutual Companies** — We only set up policy contracts with mutual companies, which means that policyholders end up with dividends. These are the opposite of stock companies—where all company profits go to stockholders.

2. **Direct vs Non-Direct Recognition Companies** — Dividends are a major boost to your policy over time, and non-direct recognition companies will pay out dividends regardless of your outstanding loans. Direct recognition companies can stifle dividends due to outstanding loans. Most of the non-direct recognition companies we use in The Money Multiplier Method have effectively delivered dividends for over a century.

3. **Policy Engineering** — Not all companies operate the same way or offer the same products. We focus on the companies with the whole life insurance policies that will work best as a banking system.

4. **Company Ratings and Investment Portfolios** — Salesmen will make this the first selling point, and

while this is important to us as well, we place the *cash flow capacity* of your policy as our number one criteria.

Obviously, insurance companies have underwriting guidelines based on their providing you with the contractual death benefit. Because we are focusing on the cash flow benefits of the policy, in some cases, a policy may need to be adjusted to fit the insurance company's guidelines or to accommodate for your health and/or your age. You can fit the minimum requirements of the death benefit by adding a temporary term rider—an option to provide additional temporary life insurance coverage—on the front end. Policies do not typically come with a term rider, so you add it in. Riders come in varying categories; some come with additional cost, and some do not.

While there can be some initial impact on the cash value early on when we add the term rider, focus on the riders that come at no additional cost and do not impact cash value. If a rider is put in place that does initially impact cash value, the benefit will far outweigh any initial cost, as the term rider is what enables you to put your policy "in force" (make it active) and begin your banking system.

Putting all the pieces together, here is how your whole life insurance policy works as a banking system:

- When you sign the contract and make your initial premium deposit with the mutual insurance company, they agree to a stated death benefit to be paid to your beneficiaries upon your "graduation" from this life.

- From the very start, your whole life insurance policy has cash value—money that you can use as collateral for loans.

- You can take out your first loan (and we suggest you do) within the first thirty days of starting your policy.

- Using your loan, pay off existing debt or use the money to fund your current expenses.

- You then repay the loan to the insurance company with interest. Treat your money as if it is that of a bank, and pay yourself back *with interest*. This interest includes the interest charge that the insurance company is charging you on the loan (which is 5% with most of our mutual companies). This interest rate charge is simple interest, so if you owe 5% on a $10,000 loan, your interest payment is $500 for the year.

- Every year, you put in your premium deposit and build cash value that you can use as collateral to take out ongoing loans.

The process of taking out loans from your policy merits some extra attention because loans are much different when you own the bank and remain in control of your money. Loans are also different than withdrawals. When you put in premium deposits, that money remains safely inside your policy, building cash value, just like when you put your money in a conventional bank. The loans you're taking from your policy come from the general fund of the insurance company, *not from your money*. The money you have put into your policy through your premium deposits always remains inside the policy, compounding and growing, and it acts as collateral for your loans.

The insurance company will lend money to you, as the owner, up to the amount of equity you have—the cash value of your policy at any point in time. Your cash value acts as collateral on the loan (from the general fund of the insurance company) and the insurance company holds a lien against any potential death benefit it has to pay.

R. Nelson Nash put this wonderfully in *Building Your Warehouse of Wealth*: "Since it is true that a policy owner can borrow up to 100% of whatever can be lent from [their] policy at any point in time, then this means that the owner has absolute and total control over the lending function of the insurance company as it relates to the equity in [their] policy."

He would have called whole life insurance, "a personal warehouse of wealth system with a death benefit as a bonus." [25]

The number one reason we use this machine is because this is what the wealthy and the elite do. It is also what banks and Fortune 100 and Fortune 500 companies do. The number one purchasers of whole life insurance in the world are conventional banks. They own more in whole life insurance than all of their land and buildings combined. Banks have quadrupled their portfolio since 2013 in terms of how much dividend-paying whole life insurance they have purchased through mutual companies.[26]

Why are banks buying so much? Because they know something the rest of us don't know—or rather, that most of us didn't know *until now*. The one thing that the wealthiest individuals and corporations use to keep control of their money, minimize taxes, and grow their money without risk is to reclaim control of the banking function. It is the one thing that you can do to achieve the same.

It is important to note that the banking system is *not* a product or an investment; it is a process and a tool. Yes, this machine helps you gain wealth, but the real magic is the process of what we're going to do to pay off debt, pay off expenses, and create cash flow.

Remember the three key principles of The Money Multiplier Method:

1. **Pay Yourself First.**
2. **Pay Yourself with Interest.**
3. **Recycle and Recapture What You Spend.**

In order to unravel your debt mess and free yourself from financial slavery, three principles are paramount to mapping out the millionaire mystery. Tony Robbins puts it well in *MONEY Master the Game*: "The 'machine' can't start working until you make the most important financial decision of your life. The decision? What portion of your paycheck you get to keep. How much will you pay yourself?"[27]

You can recycle and recapture all the money they are paying to everyone else, create real wealth, keep your money in your family, and leave the legacy you've always wanted to. Oh, and you can get all the money back from every car you will ever buy, drive, and own. It all happens when you make the decision to become the bank, set up your banking system (a specifically designed, dividend-paying whole life insurance policy), and take the loans that are available to you.

This is about adding one simple step in your financial life: controlling your environment by becoming the bank! The Money Multiplier Method can act in support of your investments, though the whole life insurance policy is designed solely to be a banking system that enables you to take care of all your financial needs—debts and expenses alike.

It's up to you to set the machine in motion, and that's exactly what we're going to help you do next so that you can get the process working for you!

The Money Multiplier Method is about how you can scale and borrow money from your whole life insurance policy. The insurance company is the administrator of your policies and you are the owner; *you* are the bank in charge of the banking system. Let's take a quick look at the players—the "all-powerful trinity"—present with the banking system: the owner, the insured, and the beneficiary.

1. **The Owner** — For the purposes of banking policies, this is the most powerful person involved in the contract. The owner has the ability to utilize the properties of this banking policy at any time he or she desires. Once the owner "goes into business" with a life insurance company through The Money Multiplier Method, the insurance company now goes to work for the owner and will begin delivering benefits on the owner's behalf. The insurance company is now the "hired help" to steward all the monetary assets. The cash value in the policy is the owner's to pay off debt or invest, etc. The owner has the power and outranks anyone else. Also, be aware that the owner may or may not be a human being. An entity like an LLC or a Trust can own a life insurance policy.

2. **The Insured** — To get a policy running, the insurance company needs a human life to assign a value to. As you can probably tell from the word itself, *life insurance* is a monetary value that gets assigned to the future economic expectancy of a person. Because the insurance company is agreeing to pay (life and death

benefits) on a person's life, they have done extensive research on tens of thousands of lives to figure out what these benefits should be. Also, the insured in a life insurance contract needs to provide a company with detail on their specific healthy body, and the company will take that data to their actuaries and underwriters and compare it to their pool of data. Once they "guess" how long the insured will live—or, more to the point, continue to make premium deposits—they will deliver the benefit numbers back to the owner.

3. **The Beneficiary** — The third person in the policy trinity is the one who is named to receive the benefits after the insured dies. The beneficiary's only responsibility is to collect the death benefit at the "graduation" of the insured person. For the banking process of The Money Multiplier Method, the beneficiary is not nearly as important to the process that we teach than the owner and the insured are. If and when any help is needed at the time of transferring the death benefit to the beneficiary, we are happy to help!

The insured can never change, but the owner and the beneficiary can change multiple times. The owner can also be the insured, or these can be different people. All three persons may assume the same or a different role in any number of additional insurance policy contracts.

There is simplicity to using the machine of whole life insurance as your banking system because the entire platform is being administrated, run, by the insurance company, and you remain the owner of the policy. Once you establish your policy with the three key players—the owner, the insured, and the beneficiary—you're in the driver's seat.

Let's set this vehicle in motion and look at just where having your own banking system can take you. Get ready to realize all that you can do with the cash flow you receive through your specifically designed whole life insurance policy.

Appreciating Depreciating Assets

At the beginning of this book, we posed two questions: *What if you could get all the money back for every purchase you've ever made? What if you could create wealth through the debts and expenses you already have?*

How much of the money that you've spent on all of the cars you've ever bought, driven, and owned do you have today? The greatest benefit you can access today from a whole life policy is using your banking system, your policy, to recapture the interest you are paying to banks and finance companies for your cars, business equipment, home renos, etc. Remember key principle #3 of The Money Multiplier Method: *Recapture what you spend.*

Think about the last car you purchased. Did you pay cash? Bank finance it? Or did you lease it? However you did it, the car purchase meant that you gave your money to the car dealer and drove away with your new vehicle. What if you had the power to recapture some, most, or all of the money you've paid for all of the cars you have bought or owned? Or, if not a car, perhaps machinery you purchased for use in your business, or remodeling costs for your home?

Here is the real magic of being your own bank: you can recapture the money you spend, even on purchases of depreciating assets like cars and machinery!

Let's look at the client example below. We're not going to get caught up in age and death benefits here. If three people of different ages—thirty, fifty, and seventy—are in the same health and all put $10,000 into their policy, the youngest will have the largest death benefit and the oldest will have the smallest. However, we aren't focused on the death benefit; we're focused on the cash available to you in your policy. If those same three people—aged thirty, fifty, and seventy—all walk into a grocery store with $20 each, who will be able to buy more groceries? None of them. They will all have the same purchasing power, so age does not matter in the conversation of cash.

In this example, the client's premium deposits are $10,000 a year, paid annually for the first seven years. When it comes to your whole life policy, you decide the premium you want to put into your policy and the frequency at which you deposit it: monthly, quarterly, or annually.

When making the decision of how much you will deposit, it is worthwhile to consider this point by R. Nelson Nash: "When you get paid for your work, you put all of it into 'someone else's bank' and then write checks from the account to buy the things of life. So 'someone else's bank' gets all of your money. If you owned a banking system, wouldn't you want to run *all* of your business through your bank?" In his book, *Becoming Your Own Banker*, he goes on to say, "If this is so, then life insurance premiums paid each year should ultimately equal annual income. . . It will take the average person about twenty years to reach this level."

In the example on the next page, our client, whom we'll call Sam Weils, is putting $10,000 a year, as premium deposits, into this policy. He decides to buy a car in year three, and in year eight, he decides to buy another one. When you buy a car using your banking system, you borrow the money from yourself and pay yourself back for the loan, plus interest, just the same as you would borrow and pay back a conventional bank.

In year three, Sam took out a loan and bought a $20,000 car. Though, let's make one point very clear; it's ideal for you to begin using the cash flow capacity of your BANK immediately by taking a loan within the first thirty days of opening your banking system, and to not stop paying the premium! Have you ever deposited too much money into your bank account? We didn't think so! The earlier you use the money in your policy, and the longer you put premiums in your policy, the larger your cash value and death benefit values are going to be.

	Using a Policy to Purchase a Car			The Money Multiplier		
Policy Year	AGE	Policy Premium Deposit	Car Loan Payment	Car Purchase	Cash Value Available	Death Benefit
1	50	$10,000			$5,811	$375,193
2	51	$10,000			$11,967	$399,724
3	52	$10,000	$4,800	$20,000	$21,187	$424,006
4	53	$10,000	$4,800		$21,392	$447,766
5	54	$10,000	$4,800		$37,211	$471,037
6	55	$4,000	$4,800		$47,718	$472,728
7	56	$4,000	$4,800		$58,391	$474,444
Total Premium & Loan Repaid: $82,000 (minus $20,000 car purchase = $62,000 net)				**Cash Value Growth: $58,391**		
8	62	$4,000	$4,800	$20,000	$49,225	$476,200
9	63	$4,000	$4,800		$60,249	$478,069
10	64	$4,000	$4,800		$71,507	$480,234
11	65	$4,000	$4,800		$83,025	$482,754
12	66	$4,000	$4,800		$94,811	$485,649
Total Premium & Loan Repaid: $44,000 (minus $20,000 car purchase = $24,000 net)				**Cash Value Growth: $45,586**		
13	67	$4,000	$4,800	$20,000	$86,877	$488,947
14	68	$4,000	$4,800		$99,236	$492,667
15	69	$4,000	$4,800		$111,912	$496,837
16	70	$4,000	$4,800		$124,909	$501,465
17	71	$4,000	$4,800		$138,244	$506,578
Total Premium & Loan Repaid: $44,000 (minus $20,000 car purchase = $24,000 net)				**Cash Value Growth: $51,367**		
18	72	$4,000	$4,800	$20,000	$131,923	$512,168
19	73	$4,000	$4,800		$145,957	$518,254
20	74	$4,000	$4,800		$160,389	$524,843
21	75	$4,000	$4,800		$175,211	$531,887
22	76	$4,000	$4,800		$190,443	$539,407
Total Premium & Loan Repaid: $44,000 (minus $20,000 car purchase = $24,000 net)				**Cash Value Growth: $58,520**		

Using a Policy to Purchase a Car: One America Whole Life 121 Policy Non - Guaranteed Values from Policy Illustration. Created January 2020.

In this example, Sam pays himself back $400 a month for five years ($4,800 a year) on his $20,000 car loan, which means that he is paying himself back $24,000. In the past, you may never have thought to pay yourself interest. You take money from your checking account, or from your savings account, or from under your mattress, but you do not pay yourself back, or with interest, for having taken out that money. Becoming your own bank is different. To live like the wealthy, you need to treat your money the same as you would treat a bank's money, and pay yourself back with interest. Remember key principle #2 of The Money Multiplier Method! If you do not pay yourself interest, you are essentially saying that your money is not as valuable as the bank's money.

Over the course of those first seven years of his policy, Sam put in $58,000 ($10,000 a year for five years and then $4,000 a year for two years) and he took out $20,000 for the car, and paid back $24,000 in car payments. He put in the $82,000 total and took out $20,000, so $62,000 is his true net injection into his banking system.

At the end of year seven he has $58,391 in cash in the account. If we divide that by the $62,000 net injection into the policy, we see that he has gotten back 94 cents on every dollar for that first car purchased! This is all done by making one simple change to his financial plan: buying a dividend paying, high premium whole life insurance policy. Cars wear out, and we will need to purchase new ones. Say that Sam decides to buy another car in year eight for $20,000 out of his cash value in the policy. He does the same thing as before and pays himself back $24,000 ($20,000 plus interest) over the course of five years.

As he continues to make premium deposits into his policy at $4,000 per year, his true net injection over years eight through twelve is $24,000 (that's $20,000 in deposits less a $20,000 car purchase in year eight, with payback of $24,000 into the policy contract). He has put back $24,000 more than he has taken out, and he has $94,811 in cash value in the policy at the end of year twelve. Look at the cash in the account: it grew from $49,225 in year eight (when he bought his second car) to $94,811 in year twelve; that is $45,586 in growth with only a $24,000 injection into the account over that five-year period, plus he bought another car.

With every car purchase, these growth numbers will continue to get bigger. Putting money into and using the whole life insurance policy as your banking system allows you to continue your normal spending habits (like buying cars) and become wealthy while you're living the life you want to live.

Over the course of the twelve years in this example, Sam's true net injection into the policy was $126,000 less the $40,000 for two cars, or $86,000 net. His cash value in year twelve is $94,811. He then has $8,811 more in the account that he put in, *and* he has two cars sitting in the driveway.

How much did the two cars cost Sam? It looks like he actually made money on the policy. While we can't say from this example that the two cars cost him $0, we can say that the scenario has Sam capitalizing on The Money Multiplier Method. This machine is about deciding to be your own banker. And while there are costs to becoming your own bank, they are negated when you dedicate yourself to this process for the long-term.

Let's revisit our initial question: Of all the cars you've ever bought, driven, or owned in your lifetime, how much of the money that you spent on them do you currently have today? Zero dollars. Going forward, if you do nothing else than get back all the money from all the cars you'll ever own, you'll be in great shape.

Consider the possibility of using this principle for other expenses in your life. This same method can work for your homes, charitable giving, and even your tax payments. When you become the bank, you can use your banking system to turn depreciating assets into appreciating assets.

It's all about how you use the machine to build your wealth. In this book, we are simply reiterating what the wealthy already know. R. Nelson Nash didn't fully invent this concept. Robert Kiyosaki didn't invent this concept. Tony Robbins didn't invent this concept. And neither did we. Insurance policies have existed for two hundred years. We simply want to teach you how to maximize an opportunity that allows you to live like the wealthy.

R. Nelson Nash would say that on March 28, 2019, he "graduated," moving from this lifetime to whatever is next for him. His teachings change the financial lives of everyone who reads them. He showed us the power of knowledge, passion, and caring. He left a legacy of truth and change, empowering us to open our minds to nonconventional thinking and solutions. He paved the way for a new kind of blueprint for financial freedom.

For every one of you reading this book, one of two things will happen:
1. You will live, or
2. You will die.

If you live, you are better off with The Money Multiplier Method. If you die, your beneficiaries receive your death benefit and are also better off . . . all because you chose to take control of your finances and use a whole life insurance policy to become your own bank.

The next question is: Are you in this for the long term?

The Marathon

A Chinese Proverb says, "The best time to plant a tree was twenty years ago. The second best time is now."

GROWING UP, BRENT WITNESSED HIS father have full direction of money coming in and going out of the family, and sometimes a windfall of money would go out just as quickly as it would come in. When Brent started his first banking system in 2011, his wife didn't believe that it was a good idea, although she did know that, like his father, Brent liked to spend money. His wife began to see the banking system as a long-term savings mechanism—a long-term machine that would force Brent to save rather than spend. He could save and still borrow to go and buy all of the things he liked.

Every year after starting his first policy, Brent added another policy, and another policy, and another policy. He began to buy at least one policy every year. Today, he has nineteen banking policies and continues to buy at least one every year. He insures his family members and those who he has a vested interest in. He owns policies on people he doesn't even have a vested interest in anymore, like chiropractors who he had sold clinics to years ago. Even though he is no longer in the chiropractic business, he still owns the policies.

Brent has also made loans to others a big part of his investment strategy. He has financed homes for each of his three children and owns the mortgage on their properties. If his kids or someone else want to borrow money to buy a $100,000 house, he lends them $75,000. They come up with the other $25,000. If they default and do not pay back the loan, he forecloses on them. He has even financed his son's pool and his cars. In doing so, he is keeping all his money in the family.

The more his kids or anyone he loans money to pays him, the more he can loan out, with the interest coming back to him and his wife. His kids get the homes and cars they want, and they are helping to fund his lifestyle with the money they are paying back, with interest. All of the money they pay back goes back into the policies and continues to get bigger—both the cash value and the death benefit. And who's going to get all the money when Brent "graduates" from this life? His kids! They are the beneficiaries on his policies. As R. Nelson Nash says, "'Plan as if you are going to live forever, and live as if you are going to die today' appears to me to be a good thought."[28]

Now, we're not here to tell you how to invest. Some of you may like stocks and bonds, while some of you may like cars, gold, silver, cryptocurrency, houses, and real estate. Brent loves to loan money to other people. What really matters is the banking function, and building everything around that.

Gimme, gimme, gimme, now, now, now—it sounds like an anthemic pop song, but it is actually the anthemic mentality sweeping the nation. We are a society that is all too familiar with instant gratification; however, as much as other investment methods can realize "instant" gains, they can also land you with instant losses. The Money Multiplier Method requires patience, strategy, and a focus on the long term.

Dividend-paying whole life insurance has provided people the time they want, the freedom they desire, and the happiness they deserve by creating wealth, not with investment strategies, but rather, with banking concepts that have been forgotten by everyone but the wealthy. But it's not just the wealthy who can use this concept. Anyone can use this strategy, as long as they understand one thing: this isn't some "get rich quick" scheme. It's a long-term commitment and requires guidance and patience.

For the first seven years of the process, "getting rich" really isn't in the picture. It's what comes after those first seven years that makes it all worthwhile because your money (your premium deposits, cash value, and death benefit) is compounding, uninterrupted, inside your policy. Albert Einstein is credited with saying, "Compound interest is the eighth wonder of the world. He who understands it, earns it. He who doesn't, pays it." In Caleb Guilliams' book, *The AND Asset: The Secret Way to Save and Use Your Money at the Same Time*, he makes this statement powerfully when he says, "If I take the wealth equation ($E=mc^2$) and put it in sentence form, it reads like this: Efficiency is multiplying your money by the use of compounding and control." Within your banking system, you have the power of uninterrupted compounding, and you are in control.

To maximize the compounding effects of your banking system, you'll want to continue to make your premium deposits in later years *and* take out new policies. Just like banks open new branches, the other policies will be your other branches, with the objective of creating a whole system of "branch office policies." R. Nelson Nash called this a "system of policies." Brent relates one's banking system to starting a new business: every year, you'll be able to take out more and more money. If you had a business that performed like that, wouldn't you want to create more of the same? That's how we approach creating a "system of policies."

Longevity and a focus on growth create legacy. When we wait to begin our policies, we are keeping wealth from our families. The Money Multiplier Method is not a new strategy; nor is it a high-risk venture. We're here to bring it to you in modern-day terms and help you build and keep the wealth you've always wanted for your family.

The rewards of a marathon can only be realized after we choose to begin the race. When you wait to start your policy (or policies), you may think that you are losing out in the present year or years, when actually, you are giving up those years at the later stages of the policy—the years when your wealth is growing at an exponential rate.

There are ten critical mistakes Infinite Banking investors sometimes make that you will want to avoid at all costs. Here's what they are:

1. **They don't think long term.** Your policy is worth more and has more cash value every single day. It's a marathon, not a sprint. Think long term, and don't get caught up in trying to get rich quick.

2. **They don't continue their education.** You've begun a banking system, and it's a process. Dive in, learn, and read—specifically *Becoming Your Own Banker* by R. Nelson Nash.

3. **They don't take loans.** Use your dollars in the system, and remember that you are never withdrawing your own cash; you are borrowing the insurance company's money.

4. **They don't use their free tools.** When you use the right tools for the job, you get the job done faster. You have access to free tools to help you get out of debt and create cash flow in your business.

5. **They don't recycle and recapture.** Principle #1 is pay yourself first. Principle #2 is pay yourself with interest. Principle #3 is recycle and recapture everything you spend. Reclaim all the money that once went out to conventional banks, mortgage companies, and creditors.

6. **They don't change their bad habits.** If you have third-party debt (or bad debt), you have the perfect process in place to leave your past behind when you become the bank. It's just a matter of beginning to think differently—of becoming your own bank.

7. **They don't put enough in.** Some people spend a lot of time trying to figure out how to put the least amount of money into their banking system. Remember that your premiums are deposits toward your wealth.

8. **They wait too long to start more policies.** Some people wait far too long to start more policies in the system. Remember that these deposits are compounding, uninterrupted, every day.

9. **They don't share the information.** The more we all know about The Money Multiplier Method and the Infinite Banking Concept™, the better off we can all be.

10. **They cancel their policies.** Nothing is worse than throwing away an asset that is growing and putting money in your pocket (providing you with cash flow).

Robert Kiyosaki says in *Second Chance: for Your Money, Your Life, and Our World*, "Anyone can take control of their financial future—if they are willing to learn, take action, make mistakes, learn from those mistakes, and remain unstoppable."

We want to save you the great pain of making mistakes and having to continuously learn from those mistakes. Remember that the machine used for The Money Multiplier Method is two hundred years old, and *you* are the only true risk in this marathon—that, and your ability to remain patient with the process. This is not a get-rich-quick scheme. This is a marathon.

This is also *not* the conventional way of thinking about money. When you control the banking function in your life, the need to finance anything you buy, the turnaround time from "zero to hero" changes. As R. Nelson Nash says, "Such a policy is engineered to get better every day, as long as the policy is in force. The earlier one starts, the longer one continues, the better the policy gets."[29]

He also says, in *Becoming Your Own Banker*, "It will take the average person at least twenty to twenty-five years to build a banking system through life insurance to accommodate all [their] own needs for finance—[their] autos, house, etc. But, once such a system is established, it can be passed on to future generations."

A whole life insurance policy is specifically designed to become more efficient every year, no matter what happens (as long as you pay your premium deposits and repay the loans you take and pay interest thereon). It takes at least three years for your banking policy to become efficient. Every year, more of every dollar you put in becomes available for you to use as cash flow, and in later years, you can take out more than you put in (available to you as cash flow). In addition, from year one, your death benefit will always be far more than the premium deposits you make.

Some people expect to put in, say, $10,000 in premium deposits right away and take out $10,000, though this isn't logical. When you put in $10,000, you can take out $6,000 (60%). You'd never deposit $10,000 into your bank account only to immediately take it all out. You can't instantly take out all of your money, and you won't instantly see significant gains in your cash value, though you also won't instantly lose your money.

Mastering the management of your debt and expenses along with mapping out the millionaire mystery takes time, and the journey begins with climbing out of the mud and up the mountain of wealth. When you find yourself in a hole, what you need to do is stop digging.

Your Debt: The Problem and Solution

The Center for Microeconomic Data's *Quarterly Report on Household Debt and Credit* reveals that total household debt increased to $13.86 trillion in the second quarter of 2019. This is the twentieth consecutive quarter that the United States has seen an increase.[30] In spite of this significant debt we have as a society, we want you to start thinking differently about loans. No longer are they a "bad thing" that you take out with third parties. Today, they become a critical component to running your own effective, long-term banking system.

Robert Kiyosaki says, "There are two kinds of debt in the world of money. They are:

1. Good debt
2. Bad debt

. . . Good debt is simply debt that makes you richer. . . . Bad debt makes the poor and middle class poorer. Bad debt is debt you pay for yourself. Good debt makes the rich richer. Good debt is debt someone else pays off for you."

Cash flow also determines if something is good or bad debt. Ask yourself if what you have purchased using debt is currently bringing in cash flow or not.

Think about how much debt you currently have. Be honest with yourself, and be specific. Think of all the bills you have. The closer you are to being fully transparent, the quicker you'll be out of debt, financially free, and "off the map"—beyond paying off your debt and into building wealth. We want you to begin to think of the marathon as beginning with your paying off all of your debts using your banking system as you build long-term wealth. The thing about Infinite Banking is that it is designed to allow you to live as you do—incurring expenses and experiencing life, or building your business to the fullest.

Brent used The Money Multiplier Map process that we'll look through in the next section. He put more money into premiums, started more policies earlier, and paid himself back more than the minimum payments on his loans. He went faster, enabling himself to pay off the nearly $1 million in thirty-nine months.

The results are contingent upon how you use your policy. Each one of you who takes out a whole life insurance policy as a banking system has certain criteria you want met. You may have debt; you may not. You may want to pay your recurring monthly bills with the banking system, or you may want to pay for vacations. If you need a new car or need to pay for your child's tuition, you may want this policy to pay for it.

What really matters is banking, and remembering that with The Money Multiplier Method of using the whole life insurance policy, you are in control; you are the bank. Build your personal debt-paying strategy, and build a team of supporters to help you. You have different financial needs than anyone else, and because of this, it's important that you find a personal money mentor, like the service we offer our clients at The Money Multiplier Method. You want an experienced supporter to help you determine the best (and fastest) possible way to reach your money goals with your banking system.

Mapping Out the Mystery

With The Money Multiplier Method, we've created a unique mapping department and system to track each individual policy owner's loans, interest, repayments, and what they recapture (when the loan is paid off). We use a proprietary MAP process—a graphical representation of your personal circumstances and financial growth. It is designed to help clients track their financial progress, build their wealth most effectively, and make the most beneficial plans when it comes to how they are using the cash flow in their policies.

The example on next page is a simplified example of how The Money Multiplier Map works. We have you disclose all of your expenses, balances, minimum payments, and interest rates. We do this because we believe not only in building the banking system, but in having a manageable system to track loans, interest, repayments, and recaptured money inside your policies.

This client, whom we'll call Sarah Sharp, came to us with twelve third-party debts. On the top of the chart are Sarah's debts. We see how much she owes, her monthly minimum payments, and how much time she has left on each loan. The total of her debt is just over $469,000. For simplicity's sake, we'll call it $450,000 in debt.

YEAR 1

Money Multiplier MAP					LLIC Heritage 2020 Whole Life Policy / Guaranteed Values Used							
Policy Month	Premium Deposit	Loan Available	Misc. Account	Total Funds Available for Use	Discover $2,348/$160 21%/18mo	Chase Card $2,650/$200 22%/15mo	Ames $2,690/$200 16%/15mo	Barclay Card $4,950/$228 29%/31mo	Lowe's $9,574/$287 11%/40mo	Nordstrom $9,783/$276 3%/38mo	Wells Fargo CC $11,251/$271 21%/75mo	Private Loan $15,355/$922 10%/19mo
			Saved									
1	$25,000	$14,611	$788	$14,611	PAID OFF	PAID OFF	PAID OFF	PAID OFF	$7,401			
2			$788									
3			$788									
4			$788									
5			$788									
6			$788									
7			$788									
8			$788									
9			$788									
10			$788									
11			$788									
12			$788									
		Remaining	$9,456									

YEAR 2

Money Multiplier MAP					LLIC Heritage 2020 Whole Life Policy / Guaranteed Values Used				
Policy Month	Premium Deposit	Loan Available	Misc. Account	Total Funds Available for Use	Lowe's $4,877/$287 11%/40mo	Nordstrom $6,720/$276 3%/26mo	Wells Fargo CC $10,270/$271 21%/63mo	Private Loan $5,377/$922 10%/7mo	BMW $17,621/$500 7.5%/40mo
			Saved						
13	$25,000	$15,144	$1,622	$24,600	PAID OFF	PAID OFF	PAID OFF		$15,498
14			$1,622						
15			$1,622						
16			$1,622						
17			$1,622						
18			$2,544					PAID OFF	
19			$2,544						
20			$2,544						
21			$2,544						
22			$2,544						
23			$2,544						
24			$2,544						
		Remaining	$25,918						

*** Debt Payoff Tool.** *LLIC Heritage 2020 Whole Life Policy Guaranteed Values Used $10,000 Base Premium & $15,000 PUA Premium Female Age 35 Standard Rating. Chart created January 2020.*

If Sarah were to pay $25,000 per year toward her debts with zero interest (we'll assume no interest), it would take her eighteen years to pay off the $450,000 in debt. The $25,000 goes into $450,000 eighteen times. Remember this number.

Instead of paying off her debt as she had in the past, Sarah started her banking system and put in $25,000 in premium deposits (in year one). There are two parts of the policy worth noting here: the base premium and the paid-up additions premium. In most policies we design, we put 40% into the base premium and the other 60% into the paid-up additions rider.

To better understand the longevity benefits of the policy, you need to understand two parts of your policy:

1. **The Paid-Up Additions Rider** — This is part of the premium, which, in the beginning stages of the policy, drives the cash value.

2. **The Base Premium** — This starts to drive the cash value as the policy becomes more matured and efficient. Later on, the paid-up additions rider is then no longer as effective and gets dropped. R. Nelson Nash always recommended paying the paid-up additions rider for as long as possible.

When a space shuttle takes off, it requires booster rockets. When it no longer needs them, they fall off. This same thing happens with your paid-up additions rider. In the beginning stages of your policy, the paid-up additions rider is what is driving the cash value. When the policy is more seasoned, the base premium drives the cash value.

Remember that *you* decide how much premium you want to put into the policy. There are no hard-and-fast rules. When we are asked how much someone should put in, we ask them, "Are you worth $2.50 an hour?" If so, that works out to $21,000 a year—the amount of annual premium deposit you can put into your policy. Remember that the faster you take out loans and the larger your premium deposits are, the greater and quicker the growth in your cash value and death benefit will be.

Let's see the impact of Sarah's premium deposits. Without changing her cash flow, taking on additional risk, or working harder, she simply invests the $25,000 into a whole life policy in her first year. She immediately borrows $14,611 (we suggested taking out her first loan within the first thirty days) and uses it to pay off her Discover, Chase, Amex, and Barclays cards and pay down her Lowe's card from $9,500 to $7,401.

Sarah then takes the money that was going to go to those first four creditors—a total of $788 a month—and pays it back to herself, into her own banking system. She is going to recapture and recycle the $788 a month, which is then available for her to use right away.

We encourage you to set up a separate checking or savings account to run the money through. You can use the one you have right now, but a separate account will help you avoid commingling the funds for tax purposes.

In year two, Sarah once again makes her $25,000 premium deposit and has $15,144 to borrow. She takes out the full $15,144 as a loan (within thirty days of the beginning of the year), and she also takes out the $9,456 that she's been paying herself back for the previous twelve months ($788 a month x twelve months), giving her a total of $24,600 to use to pay down more debt. She uses that money to pay off her Lowe's, Nordstrom, and Wells Fargo cards and to pay down her BMW debt from $17,600 to $15,498.

We then take the $788 that Sarah was paying herself back before and add in the $287 a month she was paying to Lowe's, the $276 a month she was paying to Nordstrom, and the $271 she was paying to Wells Fargo. She is now paying herself back $1,622 a month—and she is doing this without working any harder, taking on any more risk, or losing control of her finances and money. All she's doing is using her whole life insurance policy, her banking system, to pay off her debt. All she is changing is *who gets her money*. Becoming your own bank allows you to continue to live your life and spend as you do.

The private loan gets paid off organically in month eighteen, and Sarah can then pay herself $2,544 a month—the $1,622 a month she was previously paying herself, plus the $922 she was previously paying out on the private loan.

If you are reading this and feel you have no debt, you may be wondering how this can work for you. The first question is whether or not you truly have no debt. You have expenses, do you not? How comfortable would it be to live in Texas in the middle of summer without any air-conditioning, or in Colorado in the middle of winter without any heat? Even if you don't have debt, you have expenses, and recycling and recapturing your money applies to expenses as well as debt. Electric bills, cell phone bills, grocery bills, and taxes—The Money Multiplier Method works for all debt *and expenses*.

Getting back to Sarah, let's look at what happens in years three and four of her policy. At the beginning of year three, she puts in her $25,000 in premium deposit and has even more money to borrow than in the two previous years. Each and every year that you use your policy, it becomes more effective and efficient.

Sarah now has $22,549 to take out, plus what she paid herself back in the previous year, which was $25,918, for a total loan of $48,467. With her $48,467, she pays off the BMW and pays down her boat loan at West Marine from $47,000 to $8,680. She takes the money that she was paying herself back before ($2,544 a month) and adds the BMW payment of $500 a month. She can now pay herself $3,044 a month. Note: we do not deduct anything for West Marine until it is fully paid off.

In month twenty-seven, she had accumulated enough money in her miscellaneous account to eliminate the West

Marine (Boat) payment early. So she does just that, then adds the $1,261 a month that was going to West Marine and now uses that to pay herself back $4,305 per month. IT IS NOT ORGANICALLY PAID OFF!

Let's take a look back at Sarah's first three years in the policy. She put in a total of $75,000—$25,000 a year in premium deposits—and used a total of about $52,304—$14,611 borrowed in year one, $15,144 in year two, and $22,549 in year three. It would appear that she has $75,000 less $50,000, or $25,000 in her policy, but in actuality, Sarah has *all $75,000* in her policy, even though she has used $50,000 of it.

Also, remember that the loan from the insurance company is being charged with simple interest, while your dollars (or, in this case, Sarah's dollars) are growing inside the policy at uninterrupted compound interest. For example, $10,000 loaned out at 5% simple interest will cost you $500 in interest.

In a dividend-paying whole life insurance policy, you are not using your own money when you borrow money; you are using your policy as collateral and taking a loan from the general fund of the insurance company. Your own money is continuously compounding and growing, uninterrupted. This is huge. There is no other vehicle we know of that can offer these benefits.

Let's take a look at how things continue to play out for Sarah in her policy. In year four, she puts in her $25,000

YEAR 3

Policy Month	Premium Deposit	Loan Available	Misc. Account	Total Funds Available for Use	BMW $10,922/$500 7.5%/28mo	West Marine $47,136/$1,261 9%/45mo
		Money Multiplier MAP			LLIC Heritage 2020 Whole Life Policy / Guaranteed Values Used	
			Saved			
25	$25,000	$22,549	$3,044	$48,467	PAID OFF	$8,680
26			$3,044			
27			$3,044	$6,279		PAID OFF
28			$4,305			
29			$4,305			
30			$4,305			
31			$4,305			
32			$4,305			
33			$4,305			
34			$4,305			
35			$4,305			
36			$4,305			
		Remaining	$41,980			

YEAR 4

Policy Month	Premium Deposit	Loan Available	Misc. Account	Total Funds Available for Use	Condo $81,076/$1,179 6.2%/86mo		
		Money Multiplier MAP			LLIC Heritage 2020 Whole Life Policy / Guaranteed Values Used		
			Saved				
37	$25,000	$25,285	$4,305	$67,265	$13,050		
38			$4,305				
39			$4,305				
40			$4,305				
41			$4,305				
42			$4,305				
43			$4,305				
44			$4,305				
45			$4,305				
46			$4,305				
47			$4,305				
48			$4,305		PAID OFF		
		Remaining	$51,660				

__Debt Payoff Tool__. LLIC Heritage 2020 Whole Life Policy Guaranteed Values Used $10,000 Base Premium & $15,000 PUA Premium Female Age 35 Standard Rating. Chart created January 2020.

premium deposit and has $25,285 available to borrow immediately (taken out within thirty days of the beginning of the year). If she adds the $25,285 to the $41,980 she was paying herself the previous year, she has $67,265. She uses that $$67,265 to pay down her condo down from $80,076 to $13,050. Because the condo is not fully paid off, Sarah continues to pay herself $4,305 a month (the same as in year three).

Remember that you don't want to have to change your cash flow, work any harder, take any additional risk, or lose control.

At the beginning of year five, Sarah puts in her $25,000 premium deposit and has $26,170 that she can loan herself. Add that to the $51,660 she was paying herself the previous year, and she has a total of $77,830 that she can use to pay down her house from $181,421 to $102,820. Since the condo was paid off in month forty-eight, she is now paying herself $5,484 a month—$4,305 plus the $1,179 she was paying on the condo.

At the beginning of year six, Sarah puts a $10,000 premium deposit into her first policy and starts a second policy. Most clients start a second policy within the first five years. Ninety-one percent of the people we work with begin their second policy *within six months*. In starting the second policy, it is like opening a second branch of your bank.

With the deposit of just $10,000 into her initial policy, Sarah has $12,479 available to loan herself. When we talk

YEAR 5

Policy Month	Premium Deposit	Loan Available	Misc. Account	Total Funds Available for Use	House $181,421/$1,421 4.3%/171mo		
			Saved				
49	$25,000	$26,170	$5,484	$77,830	$102,820		
50			$5,484				
51			$5,484				
52			$5,484				
53			$5,484				
54			$5,484				
55			$5,484				
56			$5,484				
57			$5,484				
58			$5,484				
59			$5,484				
60			$5,484				
		Remaining	$65,808				

YEAR 6

Policy Month	1st Premium Deposit	Loan Available	2nd Premium Deposit	Loan Available	Misc. Account	Total Funds	House $91,032/$1,421 4.3%/159mo
					Saved		
61	$10,000	$12,479	$25,000	$14,611	$65,808	$92,898	PAID OFF
62							
63							
64							
65							
66							
67							
68							
69							
70							
71							
72							

__Debt Payoff Tool.__ LLIC Heritage 2020 Whole Life Policy Guaranteed Values Used $10,000 Base Premium & $15,000 PUA Premium Female Age 35 Standard Rating. Chart created January 2020.

about never wanting to stop paying premiums into your policy, this is why. That's a 30% increase on what Sarah put into the policy, available for her to use within thirty days! Wouldn't we all want our money to grow at 30%? These numbers only increase as a policy matures.

In Sarah's new, second, policy, she puts in a $25,000 premium and has $14,611 available to borrow. She adds this to the $12,479 available in her first policy, plus the $65,808 she was paying herself in that policy during the previous year, and has a grand total of $92,898 to borrow. Sarah uses that money to completely pay off her house. Her third-party debts totaling $478,000 have been *fully paid off.*

At the beginning of this example, we calculated that it would take Sarah eighteen years to pay off her debt. Using her banking system, it took just over six years. Taking a closer look, we see that Sarah put in $160,000—$25,000 in each of years one through five, plus $10,000 and $25,000 in year six—over the course of six years to pay off $478,000 in debt. She did this all without changing her cash flow, working any harder, taking on any additional risk, or losing control.

Had Sarah wanted to move faster, she could have started another policy earlier, paid herself back more, or paid more into the premium deposits. She could also have moved slower by paying less premium or paying herself back less. Brent used a similar strategy to pay off $984,711 in just thirty-nine months—the only difference was that his debts were higher and so were his premium deposits.

How fast you pay off your debt is up to you, as is how much premium you pay and how much you pay toward your debts. You make the choice to move faster or slower. Anyone can use this method. It is important that you know how to set up and use the banking system because the only risk factor in this concept is *you*, and who do you know better than yourself?

Each and every year, the cash value available in your policy will continue to go up. Continuing to make your premium deposits this year is of exponential value as your policy moves into later years because of the access to cash at a much higher rate in comparison to your deposit.

It is worthwhile for us to look at what would have happened to some of Sarah's debts had she *not* set up her banking system. Let's look at just her condo and house. In the very first year of her policy, the condo payment was $1,179 a month. When Sarah started her policy, she had 122 months left on her condo payments. To be fair, because we've been doing this for 61 months, we'll say that she still has 61 months left to pay off her condo—61 multiplied by $1,179 is $71,919.

Her house was costing her $1,421, and she had 219 months left to pay. If we subtract the 61 months that she has been in the banking system, she still has 158 months left to pay off her house. That means she owes $224,518.

Put the condo and house together, and Sarah would owe $296,437, though she now has that money inside her account, plus the growth in her policy. If Sarah is earning a 4% interest rate and she continues to pay herself back the money she agreed to pay the mortgage companies, she would have $371,708 in her pocket, plus the house, plus the condo.

Without the creation of the banking system, the banks would get all of Sarah's $371,708! This is why we need to take control of our finances and keep our money in our families.

As you continue to go through life, you are going to continue to buy and sell things. You may get a raise or get a demotion. You may come into a monetary windfall or face a downfall. When we become the bank and pay ourselves first, we master the marathon.

Cash Flow and Accumulation

We all have goals and aspirations that require cash flow. Whether you'd like to invest in real estate, pay for your child's college education, or access cash flow for monthly business expenses, mastering the marathon and maximizing your banking systems require that you know how to best manage your cash flow.

In Part II of this book, we shared an example of how you can make money by borrowing at 6% while earning 4% interest on your money in the bank. Now imagine that you have a whole life insurance policy with a guaranteed growth rate of

4% (this isn't counting any potential dividends that your policy may pay out). Say that the insurance company charges you an interest rate of 6% to take out a loan (the same rate the bank would charge you). Just the same as in the banking example, you can make money earning 4% plus potential dividends while borrowing at 6% through the ownership of a whole life policy as your banking system.

In thinking differently and shifting away from going to the bank for loans, begin to ask yourself how you can use the cash flow inside your policies to fund these goals . . . or more specifically, how you can use the cash value of our policy as collateral to take out loans to fund your dreams, goals, and needs.

Banks have strict repayment terms for loans—monthly repayments you make with them. When you are the bank, you set the schedule, the rates, and the repayment terms for your loans. You want to pay yourself back with interest, just the same as you would pay a third party if you were borrowing money from them. If you treat your money the same way you treat the bank's money, repaying your loans promptly and on time, the repayments will further fund your future and legacy building inside the policy.

If you are uncertain what interest rate you should pay yourself, make some calls to third parties and determine what the going rate is for the type of loan (car, home, business) that you are taking. Pay yourself the going rate because every percentage point of interest that you charge yourself will help your policy grow (remember the power of compounding), so don't limit the interest rate you pay yourself. You want to recapture the finance charges you would otherwise be losing if you were taking loans with third parties.

There are no fees when you borrow money from the general fund of the insurance company, though there are interest charges. The insurance company has guaranteed you (your beneficiaries) a specific death benefit value. Between now and then, they are putting your money to work. When you take a loan (from the general fund of the insurance company), the interest charge is for them lending you the money. The interest charge is never more than 6% with the mutual insurance companies we work with. Unpaid interest is added to the future loans you take, so we do recommend that you pay the interest charge.

When it comes to repaying your loan, the terms are completely up to you. You can set up a fixed repayment schedule or repay the money as you have it. There are many advantages to paying back your loans. You can rebuild your cash value in your system to use and borrow from later. You are replenishing your cash value and your death benefit. You are also restoring access to all dividend earnings when you are working with direct recognition companies—who don't always pay the full dividend when you have an outstanding loan balance. Finally, you reduce the charge you have on your interest payment.

The truth is that you don't actually have to pay back your loans, because if you have an outstanding balance, the insurance company will reduce your death benefit by the loan amount before paying out to your beneficiary. The insurance company has agreed to provide a death benefit when you put the first dollar into your policy and that is their primary focus. You can *not* repay your loan and simply continue making premium deposits. This said, we highly suggest that you do repay your loan to ensure the cash value inside your policy continues to build.

It is also important to mention that unpaid loans do *not* affect your future cash value inside the policy when your banking system is set up with a non-direct recognition insurance company. Your cash value, and how much you have available to take out as loans each year, are *not* tied to how much you borrowed or did not repay previously. You get a new sum of money to be able to take out each and every year.

The cash flow analysis tool is a simplified reconstruction of your policy contract's illustration (typically as long as twenty pages), allowing you to see how your cash values are growing year after year. Using this tool is the easiest way to see how your guaranteed growth will look and how your guaranteed growth plus dividends will look over time. This tool does not include the banking function, which will increase the cash values even more over time. Kept up to date, the cash flow analysis tool will help you track your growth and progress over the long term.

	Cash Flow Analysis					The Money Multiplier			
Age	Policy Year	Annual Premium	Guaranteed Cash Value Increase	Guaranteed Death Benefit	Guaranteed Death Benefit Increase	Projected Dividend	Projected Cash Value Per Year	Projected Death Benefit	Projected Death Benefit Increase
24	1	$12,000	$7,020	$919,078		$39	$7,059	$919,116	
25	2	$12,000	$7,282	$981,259	$62,181	$79	$7,361	$981,694	$62,578
26	3	$12,000	$7,557	$1,041,204	$59,945	$122	$7,679	$1,042,380	$60,686
27	4	$12,000	$10,462	$1,098,985	$57,781	$168	$10,630	$1,101,247	$58,867
28	5	$12,000	$12,520	$1,154,682	$55,697	$219	$12,739	$1,158,375	$57,128
29	6	$12,000	$12,982	$1,208,377	$53,695	$269	$13,251	$1,213,855	$55,480
30	7	$12,000	$13,461	$1,260,150	$51,773	$318	$13,779	$1,267,736	$53,881
31	8	$12,000	$13,960	$1,310,060	$49,910	$372	$14,332	$1,320,044	$52,308
32	9	$12,000	$14,442	$1,358,182	$48,122	$433	$14,875	$1,370,873	$50,829
33	10	$12,000	$14,898	$1,404,585	$46,403	$503	$15,401	$1,420,317	$49,444
34	11	$12,000	$15,343	$1,449,348	$44,763	$577	$15,920	$1,468,480	$48,163
35	12	$12,000	$15,835	$1,492,544	$43,196	$647	$16,482	$1,515,427	$46,947
36	13	$12,000	$16,296	$1,534,240	$41,696	$720	$17,016	$1,561,181	$45,754
37	14	$12,000	$16,811	$1,574,504	$40,264	$788	$17,599	$1,605,797	$44,616
38	15	$12,000	$17,368	$1,613,391	$38,887	$857	$18,225	$1,649,281	$43,484
39	16	$12,000	$18,003	$1,650,956	$37,565	$920	$18,923	$1,691,666	$42,385
40	17	$12,000	$18,681	$1,687,239	$36,283	$983	$19,664	$1,732,943	$41,277
41	18	$12,000	$19,394	$1,722,280	$35,041	$1,046	$20,440	$1,773,136	$40,193
42	19	$12,000	$20,154	$1,756,118	$33,838	$1,110	$21,264	$1,812,267	$39,131
43	20	$12,000	$20,957	$1,788,789	$32,671	$1,223	$22,180	$1,850,408	$38,141
44	21	$12,000	$21,764	$1,820,325	$31,536	$1,300	$23,064	$1,887,721	$37,313
45	22	$12,000	$22,599	$1,850,762	$30,437	$1,389	$23,988	$1,924,094	$36,373
46	23	$12,000	$23,432	$1,880,136	$29,374	$1,501	$24,933	$1,959,606	$35,512
47	24	$12,000	$24,268	$1,908,482	$28,346	$1,616	$25,884	$1,994,354	$34,748
48	25	$12,000	$25,128	$1,935,838	$27,356	$1,746	$26,874	$2,028,372	$34,018
49	26	$12,000	$25,987	$1,962,239	$26,401	$1,880	$27,867	$2,061,719	$33,347
50	27	$12,000	$26,842	$1,987,720	$25,481	$2,030	$28,872	$2,094,429	$32,710
51	28	$12,000	$27,677	$2,012,318	$24,598	$2,184	$29,861	$2,126,558	$32,129
52	29	$12,000	$28,523	$2,036,067	$23,749	$2,355	$30,878	$2,158,142	$31,584
53	30	$12,000	$29,329	$2,059,002	$22,935	$2,531	$31,860	$2,189,235	$31,093
Grand Total		$360,000	$548,975		$1,139,924	$29,925	$578,900		$1,270,119

Cash Flow Analysis:

* Lafayette Life Heritage 2020 Whole Life Insurance $4,800 Base Premium & $7,200 PUA Premium Female Age 24. Created January 2020.

Another added benefit that we haven't yet mentioned is that the internal growth of your policy happens *tax-free*. The Income Tax Act, as we know it today, has only been in place since 1913. Life insurance has been around for two hundred years (double the length) and is not subject to the tax code in the way that other investments are. The IRS cannot touch the money inside your whole life insurance policy because this type of policy is not a government plan sanctioned by the IRS.

When you buy a policy, you've gone into business with the insurance company. The money that you are putting into your banking system would be after-tax dollars if it's coming from your income. There is no tax on the money growing inside your policy, and, as long as you are not taking out your dividends as cash, there is no taxation on them either. Loans of the insurance company's money collateralized against the value in your policy is not subject to tax because it is not a withdrawal (only withdrawals are subject to tax). In addition, your beneficiaries will not be taxed on the death benefit. Any penalties and fees will only come into play when you are wanting to roll over your funds from a government policy into your banking system.

Throughout your life, you will have windfalls and downfalls of money. Your goals will change, and the tools you use to track your cash flow will change, making it important to evaluate your cash flow needs several times a year. Whether you make $10 an hour or $10,000 an hour, you can benefit from The Money Multiplier Method. You can break the bonds of financial slavery (that you may or may not realize you are in) and reclaim control of your own money. Without adopting the principles in this book, you are essentially stealing from yourself and your children and all the generations to come, because you are not keeping your money inside your family.

Regardless of your circumstances, The Money Multiplier Method can and will bring you wealth when used as recommended. It will take time to build wealth, but if you're in it to win it, then this concept may be just what you've been searching for.

Creating an efficient banking system with significant cash flow won't happen overnight. As R. Nelson Nash says, "Above all, you must be patient. It is going to take years to get started—and it needs to be a lifetime commitment."

Excellence is not an act but a habit. You can either have the wind at your back or in your face. Put it at your back, and you can step into the secrets of the wealthy and map out the millionaire mystery for yourself.

Let's dive into what the wealthy do differently.

The Millionaire

You and the super wealthy all have access to the same financial tools and education. The only difference is that they know how to use the tools differently.

Eight years ago, STEPHEN VINCENT and his wife were just starting out, chasing a two-year-old around and running their own business as chiropractors in Texas. They were in their late twenties and didn't have a whole lot of extra money, but what they did have, they wanted to put somewhere safe.

Stephen first met Brent at a chiropractic convention, where Brent spoke to the attendees about how he had recaptured the money he had spent. Brent got the group thinking about how anyone in the room could use the Infinite Banking Concept™

to recapture the money they've spent on both business and personal expenses.

Since he and his wife wanted a safe place to put their money, Stephen was intrigued by this financial vehicle that would allow their money to grow, tax-free, while providing them with cash flow. They had a lot of debt that they wanted to work on—student loan debt, a mortgage, and two car loans. He was not even thirty at the time and was still learning the money game. What he did know was that he didn't want to lose control of his money by putting it into the stock market, and the concept of setting himself up to be his own bank sounded incredible.

With a clear vision and passion for setting himself and his family on a path to financial freedom that not many people his age had access to, Stephen opened up his first policy with Brent, and the system started working. Soon thereafter, he opened up another policy and took one out on his wife. He started to recapture money in ways that he'd never thought possible.

At lunch, with one of his good buddies from church, Stephen excitedly mentioned his new financial process. His friend, a financial advisor, said he did the same for his clients out of his office, located three doors down from where Stephen worked. Given their proximity and longtime friendship, Stephen bought another policy on himself and one on his wife from this friend.

When he began getting statements from the policies with Brent and numbers from the other policies held with his friend, he started to question why his money he had with his friend wasn't growing as fast as the policies he had with Brent. When he questioned the lack of growth in the policies he had with his friend, his friend told him that it would take a year or more for things to get rolling. Things weren't adding up, given that his policies with Brent seemed to already be rolling.

When Stephen came to us and we looked into his other policies, we realized that they were not established in a way that allowed him to accumulate cash. The policies were set up to benefit the advisor more than Stephen. It was the opposite of what Brent had done for Stephen: set everything up in Stephen's best interest.

Stephen has since opened up five additional policies with us, for a total of seven policies. He would have never thought about opening a policy on their baby, but that's precisely what he did for his newborn, as well as his two young children. He wanted to start a small policy for each of them to build their college fund.

Knowing the price of college is "through the roof," as he says, the biggest benefit to having policies to fund his children's education is that, in spite of setting the money aside, it doesn't actually have to go to a typical college. If his ten-year-old son decides in eight years that he wants to go to a trade school and become a pipeline welder, he can do that. If he decides to go to school to become a chiropractor, the cash value of the policy will cover a good portion of the tuition. If he decides to start his own business out of high school, there is money available to help him get started.

When asked about the banking systems he has built for himself, Stephen says that he feels it is the safest place he can have his money growing, because no matter what the markets or his IRAs are doing, the money in his whole life policies stays safe and keeps growing. As for the $4,000 a month that he pays in premiums, he doesn't see it as an outlay of cash; he sees it as a deposit into his banking and his freedom.

The greatest benefit that Stephen and his wife have realized through their banking system is their ability to grow their business. They take loans out of their banking system and lend the money to their business to buy new equipment, then have their business pay them back with interest. They've also used their policy to pay taxes and have even taken a family vacation to San Diego.

He says that he feels lucky to have met Brent as a young business owner and to have access to such valuable information. To say that he has nine banks at the age of thirty-seven leaves him with a great feeling of security. He credits The Money Multiplier Method with setting them apart from other young couples and giving their kids an advantage in life, and when he talks to their ten-year-old son about money, he can tell him the *truth* about how money works.

Warren Buffet once said, "If poor people would just do what rich people do, they wouldn't be poor anymore." If a man worth billions can break it down that simply, we should be listening. We become what we repeatedly do. You and the wealthy all have the same financial tools. The only difference is that the wealthy know how to use these tools differently.

The wealthy know that money is a game, and they know the rules. Case in point, Tony Robbins called his financial-education book *MONEY Master the Game*. Since most of us didn't learn those rules at home, we continually lose the game. It's not about how much you make; it's about how much you keep. When we have more, we can do more.

The dichotomy between the wealthy and those of us who struggle to keep up with our dreams and finances changes today. Today, anyone can become his or her own banker and step into the secrets of the wealthy.

What the Wealthy Do Differently

In *MONEY Master the Game*, Tony Robbins says, "The secret to wealth is simple: find a way to do more for others than anyone else does."[31]

At The Money Multiplier, we believe that the millionaire lives in peace, gives more, and helps others. Having more than we need allows each of us to have the margin to focus on the truly important things in our lives. The banking system you create with The Money Multiplier Method helps you create the cash flow to do more, to create more, in your life and in your business.

A few years back, Chris looked at his banking system statement and was surprised to find $90,000 of cash value had accumulated in his banking system. He had more lending capacity than he personally knew what to do with, so he started loaning his money out to his students at one of his former businesses, FlipOut Academy™—a real estate education company coaching others on how to get results and create passive income through real estate.

He would loan out $40,000 here, $30,000 there, and every time it got paid back to him, he'd have that money lined up to loan to the next real estate investing student. He loaned out a lot of money at an interest rate of 12%, and every day of the week, he had a new check showing up from a loan payment. He'd put the money right back into his policy, and he did this over and over and over again.

Robert Kiyosaki says, "Financial education is learning how to harness the power of debt, because today . . . debt is money." That's an extremely powerful point: debt is money.

A lot of people look at the Infinite Banking Concept™ and think about how they are going to get rid of their debt and sail off into the sunset. The millionaire knows that once you pay off your debt, there's a whole different world on the other side. Maybe you get into real estate investing, like Chris did, or maybe you give loans to people buying your old car, like Dave Ulloa did.

You can either invest for cash flow or invest for capital gains. The banking systems you create through whole life insurance policies can be thought of as an entrepreneurial asset—an asset that can produce and provide you with cash flow—money. Whether you are an entrepreneur or not, you can make the choice to think like one. Think in terms of being the *owner* of your policies—the machines that are giving you the money and wealth you need to shape your financial future and your current personal and professional needs.

Let's take a look at just how you can fund some of the bigger-picture needs you may have, like college tuition and funding your retirement.

Funding College and Retirement

The US has more in student debt than the rest of the world combined. The latest figures point to nearly $1.5 trillion in outstanding education debt.[32] Education is becoming more expensive by the day, and our children are stepping out into the world weighed down by student debt before they even have a chance to get started in the workforce.

The good news is that you can use your banking system to fund your children's education. In this particular example, this mother, whom we'll call Kelly Long, started a policy on her ten-year-old daughter with the intention of using the policy's cash value to pay for her child's tuition fees. This is not a 529 plan, and she is not restricted to using the cash value solely for college. If her daughter decides not to go to college, Kelly can use the cash value in any way she likes, just like Stephen Vincent planned to do for his children.

In the first eight years of the policy, she contributes $10,000 in premium deposits per year. When her daughter turns eighteen, she goes off to college, though Kelly does not stop contributing to her premium deposit; she simply adjusts how much she is paying (now $4,120). When the tuition fees start in year nine, the cash value is $70,339, more than enough to cover Kelly's daughter's annual tuition of $24,000, and there is $52,339 left in cash value after the first year of Kelly's daughter's annual tuition.

Since Kelly knows the value of paying herself back and wants to teach her daughter to treat her money as she would a bank's money, she helps her daughter pay back the $6,000 a year into the policy (an amount that doesn't put too big of a strain on her daughter's finances). As her daughter begins to work more, she increases her repayment amount to $15,000 a year. The loan is completely repaid by year seventeen and can be used for anything else.

Over the course of twenty-five years, with a total of $150,040 in premium deposits and a total tuition cost of $96,000, a

Using a Policy Contract to Pay for College			The Money Multiplier			
Policy Year	Age	Policy Premium Deposit	Repayment To Self	School Bill	End of Year Cash Value Available	Death Benefit
1	10	$10,000			$5,298	$1,135,495
2	11	$10,000			$11,211	$1,219,982
3	12	$10,000			$17,442	$1,302,796
4	13	$10,000			$24,002	$1,383,824
5	14	$10,000			$31,645	$1,463,157
6	15	$10,000			$42,033	$1,541,255
7	16	$10,000			$52,820	$1,618,112
8	17	$10,000			$64,085	$1,693,978
9	18	$4,120	$6,000	$24,000	$52,339	$1,704,914
10	19	$4,120	$6,000	$24,000	$40,899	$1,716,377
11	20	$4,120	$6,000	$24,000	$29,792	$1,728,447
12	21	$4,120	$6,000	$24,000	$18,982	$1,741,056
13	22	$4,120	$15,000		$41,485	$1,753,882
14	23	$4,120	$15,000		$64,314	$1,766,915
15	24	$4,120	$15,000		$87,503	$1,780,117
16	25	$4,120	$15,000		$111,095	$1,793,844
17	26	$4,120	$12,000		$132,139	$1,808,196
18	27	$4,120			$141,611	$1,823,416
19	28	$4,120			$151,538	$1,839,529
20	29	$4,120			$159,897	$1,856,518
21	30	$4,120			$170,710	$1,874,069
22	31	$4,120			$181,983	$1,892,152
23	32	$4,120			$193,731	$1,910,638
24	33	$4,120			$205,984	$1,929,823
25	34	$4,120			$218,751	$1,950,051
Total Premium:$150,040 / School Cost: $96,000				Cash Value Growth: $218,751		

Using a Policy Contract to Pay for College. One America Whole Life 121 Non-Guaranteed Cash Values From Policy Illustration. Created January 2020. The rates and numbers may change with dividend and interest rate changes.

traditional bank account would have only $54,040 remaining ($150,040 minus $96,000). Not this policy! This policy has $218,751 in cash value available for Kelly's daughter to use.

Outside of paying for your child's or children's education, another added benefit to using a whole life insurance policy as your banking system is funding your own retirement.

In this example, our client, whom we'll call Margo, started her policy at forty years of age. Given that her focus was on retirement, she chose not to use the banking function even once with this policy. Had she done so, the values on the policy would have been even higher (so we highly recommend always using the banking function).

Margo received an increasing annual dividend (bonus) every year, beginning at age forty-two. At year twenty-one of the policy, when Margo turned sixty, she changed the policy by surrendering the cash value of her paid-up additions only. This income is tax-free until the amount withdrawn equals the premium deposits. So every year for fifteen years, Margo was able to draw $26,666 to fund her retirement. If she is still alive at that time, she will have $419,421 in cash value that she can start utilizing tax-free to continue enjoying her retirement lifestyle.

In the following alternative example, Margo decided to use some of her cash value in addition to the cash value of her paid-up additions, so she has a higher amount to take home

Using a Policy Contract to Fund Your Retirement			The Money Multiplier			
Policy Year	Age	Policy Premium Deposit	Cumulative Guaranteed Cash Value	Annual Dividend	Passive Income In Retirement	Death Benefit
1	40	$20,000	$10,564	$2		$1,219,638
2	41	$20,000	$27,345	$173		$1,219,638
3	42	$20,000	$44,776	$331		$1,219,638
4	43	$20,000	$63,096	$631		$1,219,638
5	44	$20,000	$82,268	$849		$1,219,638
6	45	$20,000	$102,423	$1,139		$1,219,638
7	46	$20,000	$123,577	$1,388		$1,219,638
8	47	$20,000	$145,790	$1,664		$1,219,638
9	48	$20,000	$169,106	$1,961		$1,219,638
10	49	$20,000	$193,566	$2,273		$1,219,638
11	50	$20,000	$219,262	$2,648		$1,219,638
12	51	$20,000	$246,251	$3,032		$1,219,638
13	52	$20,000	$274,584	$3,434		$1,219,638
14	53	$20,000	$304,348	$3,893		$1,219,638
15	54	$20,000	$335,617	$4,376		$1,219,638
16	55	$20,000	$368,487	$4,879		$1,219,638
17	56	$20,000	$402,741	$5,139		$1,244,001
18	57	$20,000	$438,407	$5,404		$1,292,055
19	58	$20,000	$475,555	$5,696		$1,339,291
20	59	$20,000	$514,231	$5,986		$1,385,795
21	60	$0	$509,977	$5,961	$26,666	$1,329,409
22	61	$0	$505,458	$5,955	$26,666	$1,274,796
23	62	$0	$500,659	$5,945	$26,666	$1,221,939
24	63	$0	$495,606	$5,984	$26,666	$1,170,758
25	64	$0	$490,281	$6,004	$26,666	$1,121,303
26	65	$0	$484,678	$6,030	$26,666	$1,073,461
27	66	$0	$478,787	$6,039	$26,666	$1,027,181
28	67	$0	$472,608	$6,055	$26,666	$982,363
29	68	$0	$466,117	$6,054	$26,666	$938,965
30	69	$0	$459,303	$6,067	$26,666	$896,897
31	70	$0	$452,145	$6,089	$26,666	$854,134
32	71	$0	$444,617	$6,108	$26,666	$816,639
33	72	$0	$436,667	$6,119	$26,666	$778,354
34	73	$0	$428,288	$6,139	$26,666	$741,209
35	74	$0	$419,421	$6,129	$26,676	$705,168
Totals		$400,000		$145,576	$400,000	

Using a Policy Contract to Fund Your Retirement: One America Whole Life Select Life Insurance Female Age 40. Created January 2020. The rates and numbers may change with dividend and interest rate changes.

		Using a Policy Contract to Fund Your Retirement			The Money Multiplier	
Policy Year	Age	Policy Premium Deposit	Cumulative Guaranteed Cash Value	Annual Dividend	Passive Income In Retirement	Death Benefit
1	40	$20,000	$10,564	$2		$1,219,638
2	41	$20,000	$27,345	$173		$1,219,638
3	42	$20,000	$44,776	$331		$1,219,638
4	43	$20,000	$63,096	$631		$1,219,638
5	44	$20,000	$82,268	$849		$1,219,638
6	45	$20,000	$102,423	$1,139		$1,219,638
7	46	$20,000	$123,577	$1,388		$1,219,638
8	47	$20,000	$145,790	$1,664		$1,219,638
9	48	$20,000	$169,106	$1,961		$1,219,638
10	49	$20,000	$193,566	$2,273		$1,219,638
11	50	$20,000	$219,262	$2,648		$1,219,638
12	51	$20,000	$246,251	$3,032		$1,219,638
13	52	$20,000	$274,584	$3,434		$1,219,638
14	53	$20,000	$304,348	$3,893		$1,219,638
15	54	$20,000	$335,617	$4,376		$1,219,638
16	55	$20,000	$368,487	$4,879		$1,219,638
17	56	$20,000	$402,741	$5,139		$1,244,001
18	57	$20,000	$438,407	$5,404		$1,292,055
19	58	$20,000	$475,555	$5,696		$1,339,291
20	59	$20,000	$514,231	$5,986		$1,385,795
21	60	$0	$486,643	$5,961	$50,000	$1,329,409
22	61	$0	$482,124	$5,955	$50,000	$1,274,796
23	62	$0	$477,325	$5,945	$50,000	$1,221,939
24	63	$0	$472,272	$5,984	$50,000	$1,170,758
25	64	$0	$466,947	$6,004	$50,000	$1,121,303
26	65	$0	$461,344	$6,030	$50,000	$1,073,461
27	66	$0	$455,453	$6,039	$50,000	$1,027,181
28	67	$0	$449,274	$6,055	$50,000	$982,363
29	68	$0	$442,783	$6,054	$50,000	$938,965
30	69	$0	$435,969	$6,067	$50,000	$896,897
31	70	$0	$428,811	$6,089	$50,000	$854,134
32	71	$0	$421,283	$6,108	$50,000	$816,639
33	72	$0	$413,333	$6,119	$50,000	$778,354
34	73	$0	$404,954	$6,139	$50,000	$741,209
35	74	$0	$396,087	$6,129	$50,000	$705,168

Using a Policy Contract to Fund Your Retirement: One America Whole Life Select Life Insurance Female Age 40. Created January 2020. The rates and numbers may change with dividend and interest rate changes.

every year in retirement: $50,000. She also has a $705,168 death benefit to pass on to her family.

Funding with Your Home Equity Line

As we mentioned earlier, using your whole life insurance policy as a banking system is not an investment; it is a process that fits into your bigger financial picture. As you look at your biggest financial picture, you have the option to use your home equity line of credit (HELOC) to fund your banking system. A HELOC is a loan from a mortgage company or bank in which the lender agrees to lend a maximum amount within an agreed-upon term, using the borrower's equity in his or her home as collateral for the loan. Using a HELOC is something that most people do not do with their first policy . . . usually because they do not realize that doing so is even a possibility.

In the example on the following page, our client, whom we'll call Jane Rutledge, has a HELOC with $150,000 available to use. For any monies she takes out of the HELOC, she is charged 5% interest.

Jane decided to start a policy with a $50,000 annual premium deposit. To pay this amount, she pays $20,000 out of pocket, and the other $30,000 comes from the HELOC. She does this same split for five years, until she has exhausted all cash available in the HELOC ($150,000).

The whole life insurance policy begins producing cash right away, which she uses to cover the HELOC interest. In

		Using a HELOC to Fund a Policy Contract			The Money Multiplier				
Age	Policy Year	Out Of Pocket Funds	HELOC Funds	Annual Premium to Insurance Company	Guaranteed Cash Value Per Year	Annual Dividend	HELOC Interest	Net Growth Per Year	Cumulative Growth
35	1	$20,000	$30,000	$50,000	$29,215	$176	-$1,500	$27,715	$27,715
36	2	$20,000	$30,000	$50,000	$30,241	$362	-$3,000	$27,241	$54,956
37	3	$20,000	$30,000	$50,000	$35,643	$551	-$4,500	$31,143	$86,099
38	4	$20,000	$30,000	$50,000	$49,588	$745	-$6,000	$43,588	$129,687
39	5	$20,000	$30,000	$50,000	$51,367	$936	-$7,500	$43,867	$173,554
40	6	$20,000		$20,000	$24,097	$958	-$7,500	$16,597	$190,151
41	7	$20,000		$20,000	$25,058	$981	-$7,500	$17,558	$207,709
42	8	$20,000		$20,000	$26,083	$1,004	-$7,500	$18,583	$226,292
43	9	$20,000		$20,000	$27,169	$1,070	-$7,500	$19,669	$245,961
44	10	$20,000		$20,000	$28,235	$1,103	-$7,500	$20,735	$266,696
45	11	$20,000		$20,000	$29,344	$1,144	-$7,500	$21,844	$288,540
46	12	$20,000		$20,000	$30,456	$1,204	-$7,500	$22,956	$311,496
47	13	$20,000		$20,000	$31,520	$1,264	-$7,500	$24,020	$335,516
48	14	$20,000		$20,000	$32,631	$1,334	-$7,500	$25,131	$360,647
49	15	$20,000		$20,000	$33,718	$1,405	-$7,500	$26,218	$386,865
50	16	$20,000		$20,000	$34,798	$1,486	-$7,500	$27,298	$414,163
51	17	$20,000		$20,000	$35,853	$1,567	-$7,500	$28,353	$442,516
52	18	$20,000		$20,000	$36,855	$1,659	-$7,500	$29,355	$471,871
53	19	$20,000		$20,000	$37,824	$1,753	-$7,500	$30,324	$502,195
54	20	$20,000		$20,000	$38,785	$1,858	-$7,500	$31,285	$533,480
55	21	$20,000		$20,000	$39,864	$1,961	-$7,500	$32,364	$565,844
56	22	$20,000		$20,000	$40,983	$2,068	-$7,500	$33,483	$599,327
57	23	$20,000		$20,000	$42,198	$2,186	-$7,500	$34,698	$634,025
58	24	$20,000		$20,000	$43,449	$2,314	-$7,500	$35,949	$669,974
59	25	$20,000		$20,000	$44,727	$2,445	-$7,500	$37,227	$707,201
60	26	$20,000		$20,000	$46,018	$2,577	-$7,500	$38,518	$745,719
61	27	$20,000		$20,000	$47,225	$2,721	-$7,500	$39,725	$785,444
62	28	$20,000		$20,000	$48,461	$2,878	-$7,500	$40,961	$826,405
63	29	$20,000		$20,000	$49,644	$3,036	-$7,500	$42,144	$868,549
64	30	$20,000		$20,000	$50,849	$3,207	-$7,500	$43,349	$911,898
Grand Totals		$600,000	$150,000	$750,000	$1,121,898	$47,951		$911,898	

Using a Policy Contract to Fund Your Retirement: One America Whole Life Select Life Insurance Cash Value Used at Age 61. Created January 2020. The rates and numbers may change with dividend and interest rate changes.

the net growth column, you can see how much remains even after she has paid the HELOC interest. After five years, the cumulative growth column shows that she has more than enough money as cash value to pay the HELOC down to zero, stopping the interest charge.

In year six, Jane already has cash values in excess of her premium deposits, which she can begin using to pay down her debt and cover her expenses while building wealth inside her policy.

Funding your child's or children's education, funding your retirement, and drawing from your HELOC to build your banking system are all innovative ways that you can use The Money Multiplier Method to begin to live like the wealthy.

These are not complicated strategies, but rather, a new way of thinking about existing products and processes, and how we can bridge them together to reclaim control of our finances and free ourselves from the financial slavery of taking out loans and paying back debts to third parties. Robert Kiyosaki says, "The Generalized Principle of the rich is the principle of *ephemeralization* . . . In the simplest of terms, it means 'to do more with less.'"[33]

In the first chapter of this book, we began with the premise of *doing one thing differently* to change the course of your financial future. The concept of becoming your own bank is simple; it is one that allows you to do so much more with the money you have. It also awakens you to just how much you *do* have. This all comes back to thinking differently. When you begin to think like the wealthy, you are shaping the course of your financial destiny.

Remember, you and the super wealthy all have access to the same financial tools and education. The only difference is that they know how to use the tools differently. This is your money and your financial life. Long-term changes require that you start making changes today to think differently about your money and step into the secrets and strategies of the wealthy. This is the movement we want to help create.

The Movement

*The concept of becoming your own bank is simple; it is one that
allows you to do so much more with the money you have.*

I N 2006, WHEN LIFE AS a financial advisor was treating Chris
very well, he heard about the concept of flipping houses and
decided that would be his next venture. A Realtor he knew
found him a house out in Gasport, New York that was ripe
for flipping. He and his best, longtime dirt-bike-riding-friend
Mike decided to take the leap together. Chris would put the
money in, and Mike would do the renovation work.

Diving into this new venture, Chris naively thought the
bank was going to give him all the money he needed to buy
and renovate the house. He had already bought a house, his

personal residence, and had gotten almost 95% of the money he'd needed. He thought the same was going to happen with an investment property. When he got the commitment letter from the bank, his first thought was, *something's wrong with these numbers.*

The bank explained to Chris that they could only lend him 80% of the purchase price because the house was not his primary residence. He had two choices: he could either abandon the dream of flipping this house, or he could figure it out. He chose option B.

When thinking of where he could get the money he needed for the down payment on the house, Chris knew that he could take a loan from his 401(k), and he did that, but was still short. Then he remembered that he had a whole life insurance policy. Three years prior, he had started his first policies and had built up cash value, so he was then able to take out loans from two policies—just enough to get the house and pay for most of the renovations. Borrowing from his existing life insurance policy was not Infinite Banking; he just knew that he could take loans from life insurance policies.

Had Chris known about how Infinite Banking policies were built, he would have built his savings vehicles differently and had way more money . . . not to mention been able to recapture all the money he was spending on his renovation. Nevertheless, that life insurance policy got him that first house.

He sold the house, paid the insurance policy loans back, and started buying more real estate. He took loans from his life insurance plans and from his 401(k) over and over and over again. For every real estate deal and for his business, he borrowed the money he needed and he paid it back. Then in 2014, he implemented The Money Multiplier Method and began truly building his wealth and cash flow with this banking system.

Using The Money Multiplier Method for real estate deals allowed Chris to scale his business to a total of over two hundred flips after recovering from losing nearly everything in the 2008 market crash.

He was good with his money, very good at private money, and great with Infinite Banking. When he saw a deal he wanted to be a part of, he would go to the bank and take out a loan, and then use his own banking system to pay the 20% plus closing costs and renovation costs. In doing so, he'd write a note (like a promissory note) to his business—his LLC—from his banking policy. Once he finished the renovation, he'd rent it out and pay the rent back to himself. Through this process, he built his banking system at an exponential rate, taking money out and repeating his home-buying and renovation process again and again.

Tony Robbins says, "You have to make the shift from being a consumer in the economy to becoming an owner—and you do it by becoming an investor."[34] Chris learned how to become an investor in his own properties and in the properties of his real estate investing students. His process and business were so successful that they landed him a pilot on HGTV called *Risky Builders.*

The stories we've shared in this book—ours and those of our clients—illustrate the extent to which (significant) debts can be paid off, expenses can be covered, and investment opportunities can be captured using the cash flow capacity of your banking system.

What matters is that you *start today.* Remember that the years lost are not the ones you spend waiting to get started, but rather, the later years of your policy, when your money is compounding at an even greater rate. You owe this to yourself to relieve the pressure of the mounting debt and expenses in your business and personal life, and you owe it to your family to keep your wealth there . . . all without giving away control of your financial future and unnecessarily assuming all of the added risk that comes along with other investments.

Now that you know how money really works, how the banks work, and how you can capitalize on the bank's strategies to ensure that the old ways of thinking are no longer costing you your financial future, it's time to get started. It's time to step into the secrets of the wealthy, to internalize this outside-the-box thinking, and to begin to live out the millionaire mystery in your life.

Get on the backward bicycle, master riding it, and stop doing what everyone else is doing. Form your own line to the bathroom. Choose to control the environment in which you operate and live by becoming your own bank. Doing so has exponentially altered the course of our lives, and we trust that it will do the same for you.

Client Testimonials

"Instead of going out and getting loans and paying interest—paying other people, like the banks—when you structure things [with The Money Multiplier Method], all of your money stays in the family. In America, they won't teach you this in high school, and they won't teach you this in college. Most people in the industry where this is found won't tell you about it. I have a great friend in Brent Kesler, who is a master at this. Five years ago, he taught me what completely changed the course of our lives."

— Dave Ulloa, California

"The concept of Infinite Banking, introduced to us by Brent Kesler, allowed my family to attack our overwhelming debts at a rapid pace. We can't thank him enough for his financial guidance and thorough knowledge of the concept."

— Tré Kirkland, South Carolina

"Brent saved my life! Financial freedom is very important, especially in today's time. If it weren't for him and his expertise, I would be living below the poverty line! With his help, I was able to buy a house, a long-lost dream that became a reality!"

— *Samara McKnight, Oklahoma*

"Brent Kesler is the real deal, and he has changed our financial life forever and the legacy that we will leave with our precious daughter and her family and eventual children and grandchildren one day, when we 'graduate.'"

— *Carly Carney, Colorado*

About the Authors

BRENT KESLER

Every day, The Money Multiplier founder Brent Kesler is helping individuals free themselves from financial slavery, take control of their own financial lives, and create massive wealth for their families.

After fourteen years as a chiropractor and chiropractic coach, Brent had racked up nearly $1 million in third-party debt. Upon implementing The Money Multiplier (TMM) Method, he paid off every penny in three years and became deeply passionate about how powerful The Money Multiplier Method truly is. As he began to share it with others, they immediately wanted to join the program, and Brent became a licensed producer.

After five years of working as an agent at other firms, Brent founded The Money Multiplier, LLC, in 2017. His main goal is to help more people understand how to manage and grow their wealth. In addition to serving his clients one-to-one, he has educated thousands of people around the country on the dynamics of the TMM Method and how money really works.

CHRIS NAUGLE

Chris Naugle has dedicated his life to being America's #1 Money Mentor. His success includes managing over $30 million in assets in the financial services and advisory industry and tens of millions of dollars in real estate business, with over 260 transactions since 2014 and an HGTV pilot.

In twenty years, Chris has built and owned sixteen companies, with his businesses being featured in Forbes, on ABC, and on *House Hunters.* He is the cofounder and CEO of FlipOut Academy™, founder of The Money School™, and a Money Mentor for The Money Multiplier.

As an innovator and visionary in wealth-building and real estate, he empowers entrepreneurs, business owners, and real estate investors with the knowledge of how money works. Innovating what it takes to break the chains of financial slavery, Chris is driven to deliver the financial knowledge that fuels lasting freedom. To date, he has spoken to and taught over ten thousand Americans.

For more information, visit our website:

https://themoneymultiplier.com/

Get started with the 10-Part Training Video:

https://themoneymultiplier.com/member-area/

Watch our webinar:

https://moneyschoolrei.com/tmmm

For additional training and tools, check out:

www.Thecashcompound.com/bankwithus

Endnotes

1   R. Nelson Nash, *Becoming Your Own Banker: Unlock the Infinite Banking Concept*, Infinite Banking Concepts, 2009.

2   R. Nelson Nash, *Becoming Your Own Banker: Unlock the Infinite Banking Concept*, Infinite Banking Concepts, 2009.

3   Robert Kiyosaki, *Second Chance: For Your Money, Your Life, and Our World*, Plata Publishing, 2015.

4   U.S. Government Accountability Office, "Understanding the Debt," https://www.gao.gov/americas_fiscal_future?t=federal_debt.

5   R. Nelson Nash, *Becoming Your Own Banker: Unlock the Infinite Banking Concept*, The Infinite Banking Concepts, 2009.

6   Trading Economics, "United States Personal Savings Rate" https://tradingeconomics.com/united-states/personal-savings.

7   Tony Robbins, *MONEY Master the Game: 7 Simple Steps to Financial Freedom*, Simon & Schuster, 2014, page 3.

8   Tony Robbins, *MONEY Master the Game: 7 Simple Steps to Financial Freedom*, Simon & Schuster, 2014, page 4.

9   Robert Kiyosaki, *Second Chance: For Your Money, Your Life, and Our World*, Plata Publishing, 2015, page 8-9.

10 Bob Pisani, CNBC, "Baby boomers face retirement crisis — little savings, high health costs and unrealistic expectations," April 2019 https://www.cnbc.com/2019/04/09/baby-boomers-face

-retirement-crisis-little-savings-high-health-costs-and-unrealistic-expectations.html.

11 Annie Nova, CNBC, "Baby boomers face more risks to their retirement than previous generations," November 7, 2018 https://www.cnbc.com/2018/11/07/one-third-of-baby-boomers-had-nothing-saved-for-retirement-at-age-58-.html.

12 Ben Steverman, Bloomberg, "Half of Older Americans Have Nothing in Retirement Savings," March 26, 2019 https://www.bloomberg.com/news/articles/2019-03-26/almost-half-of-older-americans-have-zero-in-retirement-savings.

13 Tony Robbins, *MONEY Master the Game: 7 Simple Steps to Financial Freedom*, Simon & Schuster, 2014, page 6.

14 Robert Kiyosaki, *Second Chance: For Your Money, Your Life, and Our World*, Plata Publishing, 2015, page 317.

15 Robert Kiyosaki, *Second Chance: For Your Money, Your Life, and Our World*, Plata Publishing, 2015, page 317.

16 Robert Kiyosaki, *Second Chance: For Your Money, Your Life, and Our World*, Plata Publishing, 2015.

17 Robert Kiyosaki, *Second Chance: For Your Money, Your Life, and Our World*, Plata Publishing, 2015, page 142. "All rates are solely an example and not indicative of exactly what you will pay. "Rates shown are for example purposes only. They do not reflect actual rates charged or received.

20 bauerfinancial.com.

21 "A record 7 million Americans are 3 months behind on their car payments, a red flag for the economy," The Washington Post, February 12, 2019, https://www.washingtonpost.com/business/2019/02/12/record-million-americans-are-months-behind-their-car-payments-red-flag-economy/.

22 R. Nelson Nash, *Becoming Your Own Banker: Unlock the Infinite Banking Concept*, Infinite Banking Concepts, 2009, page 17. "This seems to be the current situation that doesn't change all much."

23 Tony Robbins, *Money: Master the Game: 7 Simple Steps to Financial Freedom*, Simon & Schuster, 2014, page 50.

24 R. Nelson Nash, *Building Your Warehouse of Wealth*, Infinite Banking Concept™, LLC, 2000 (2012).

25 R. Nelson Nash, *Building Your Warehouse of Wealth, Infinite Banking Concepts, 2000 (2012)*.

26 FDIC, fdic.gov and Barry James Dyke, *The Pirates of Manhattan*, Castle Asset Management, LLC, 2012.

27 Tony Robbins, *MONEY Master the Game: 7 Simple Steps to Financial Freedom*, Simon & Schuster, 2014, page 56

28 R. Nelson Nash, *Becoming Your Own Banker: Unlock the Infinite Banking Concept*, Infinite Banking Concepts, 2009.

29 R. Nelson Nash, *Building Your Warehouse of Wealth,* Infinite Banking Concept™, LLC, 2000 (2012).

30 Federal Reserve Bank of New York, "Household Debt and Creditor Report," https://www.newyorkfed.org/microeconomics/hhdc.html.

31 Tony Robbins, *MONEY Master the Game: 7 Simple Steps to Financial Freedom*, Simon & Schuster, 2014, page 6

32 Bloomberg, "Student Debt," https://www.bloomberg.com/quicktake/student-debt.

33 Robert Kiyosaki, *Second Chance: For Your Money, Your Life, and Our World*, Plata Publishing, 2015, page 134

34 Tony Robbins, *MONEY Master the Game: 7 Simple Steps to Financial Freedom*, Simon & Schuster, 2014, page 6.